On the Road Again

AMERICAN ALLIANCE OF MUSEUMS

The American Alliance of Museums has been bringing museums together since 1906, helping to develop standards and best practices, gathering and sharing knowledge, and providing advocacy on issues of concern to the entire museum community. Representing more than 35,000 individual museum professionals and volunteers, institutions, and corporate partners serving the museum field, the Alliance stands for the broad scope of the museum community.

The American Alliance of Museums' mission is to champion museums and nurture excellence in partnership with its members and allies.

Books published by AAM further the Alliance's mission to make standards and best practices for the broad museum community widely available.

On the Road Again

Developing and Managing Traveling Exhibitions

Second Edition

R EBECCA A. B UCK, J EAN A LLMAN G ILMORE, AND I RENE T AURINS

ROWMAN & LITTLEFIELD

Lanham • Boulder • New York • London

Published by Rowman & Littlefield
An imprint of The Rowman & Littlefield Publishing Group, Inc.
4501 Forbes Boulevard, Suite 200, Lanham, Maryland 20706
www.rowman.com

6 Tinworth Street, London SE11 5AL, United Kingdom

British Library Cataloguing in Publication Information Available

Library of Congress Cataloging-in-Publication Data

Library of Congress Control Number: 2020903067
ISBN: 978-1-5381-3076-6 (cloth)
ISBN: 978-1-5381-3077-3 (pbk.)
ISBN: 978-1-5381-3078-0 (electronic)

Exhibitions which travel have become more and more popular, particularly during the last two decades, and since the war in 1945 this activity has increased and spread internationally. While its development has taken place recently, the idea is over a century old and its originator one of the leading museums of Great Britain, the Victoria and Albert in London. . . . The prototype in England was launched in 1850 with loans of works of art from the original Victoria and Albert to the Central School of Design at Somerset House, and during the following two years the exhibition was successively shown at various provincial schools.

—Elodie Courter Osborn, *Manual of Travelling Exhibitions*, 1953

Contents

Acknowledgments

First-edition authors Rebecca Buck and Jean Gilmore are pleased and grateful that Irene Taurins joined us for the production of this second edition of *On the Road Again*, lending her wealth of wisdom and knowledge of current daily operations to a pair of retired registrars. The three of us heartily thank those who wrote new articles for this edition: Jacqueline Cabrera, Cabrera + Art + Management; Patricia Loiko, National Endowment for the Arts; and Katherine Steiner, The Mint Museum. John E. Simmons, Museologica, was instrumental in convincing Rowman & Littlefield to publish a second edition of the book and contributed many new entries to the bibliography.

In addition, a number of knowledgeable, generous persons reviewed articles, offered advice, noted needed changes, amended text, answered questions, and otherwise lent their expertise to bringing this book up to date: Lynne Addison, Yale University Art Gallery; Eric Fischer, Willis Fine Art, Jewelry & Specie; David Gal-lagher, Philadelphia Museum of Art; Heather Hope Kuruvilla, MA, JD, Kutztown University of Pennsylvania; Michele Leopold, The Mint Museum; Jeff Minett, AON Huntington T. Block; John O'Halloran, Masterpiece International; Suzanne Quigley, Art & Artifact Services; John Robinette, J. T. Robinette, LLC; and Suzanne Wells, Philadelphia Museum of Art.

We reiterate our gratitude to the many individuals whose knowledge, expertise, and assistance contributed to the first edition, much of which persists in the current volume. Many thanks to Charles Harmon, Erinn Slanina, and their colleagues at Rowman & Littlefield for their help in bringing this edition of *On the Road Again: Developing and Managing Traveling Exhibitions* to fruition.

Rebecca A. Buck
Jean Allman Gilmore
Irene Taurins

CHAPTER 1

Introduction

Things have changed since the first edition of this book was published in 2003. The American Association of Museums is now the American Alliance of Museums (AAM); the Registrars' Committee (RC-AAM) has been integrated with art handlers of the former Packing and Crating Information Network-Professional Interest Committee (PACIN-PIC) into the Collections Stewardship Professional Network. AAM now offers, as well, a Traveling Exhibition Network (TEN). A new professional group, the Association of Registrars and Collection Specialists (ARCS) and an expanded collections group Packing, Art Handling, and Collections Care Information Network (PACCIN), have formed independent organizations and flourished.

The creation and implementation of traveling exhibitions remains complicated. Each exhibition has its own characteristics. Exhibitions comprised of organizer-owned collections are the simplest, but the time to produce them must include conservation checks and photography, as well as label production, design, crate building, insurance and transport arrangements, and creation of condition, packing, design, and installation books. Loan collections, or a combination of owned and loaned objects, may be specified, but six months or more should be added to the time necessary to do a thorough job. There may or may not be a publication, but add a year if there is one! Indemnity may be sought, so add two years if it is! Remember to take into consideration that department or person who always runs late before you even begin.

Some things have become a bit easier since the first edition; condition reporting with tablets and digital photography is a wonderful development. Most of the computer programs we now use in museums are more sophisticated than previous ones and allow exhibition management through their platforms. The biggest issues, such as the money needed for timely conservation, state-of-the art crates, interactive devices, as well as travel and publicity, remain a great challenge for each institution with a traveling exhibition program. In this edition we have updated resource information and information that was time-limited. In doing that, we found that many of the basics, such as contracts, budgets, and time lines, stay relatively constant.

Our purpose continues to be the same: present small and midsized museums and new museum personnel with basic information that can help them create and circulate an exhibition successfully. We address personnel in small to midsized museums who are charged with producing and managing a traveling exhibition for the first time. Our personal perspectives come from art and anthropology museums, but we hope we have included enough general information to allow those in other disciplines to derive insight and expertise. We do not cover hands-on or children's exhibitions, which share some characteristics with traditional traveling exhibitions but have considerable differences that merit exploration elsewhere.

There are other resources to turn to; many of the published ones are listed in the selected bibliography. In addition, there are commercial exhibition services that work with museums to realize the circulation of existing exhibitions. We hope the text, checklists, forms, and sample contracts contained herein will come to your aid when the task of circulating an exhibition seems overwhelming. Think of us as you tool down the road in an eighteen-wheeler, and we will do the same for you.

Rebecca A. Buck
Jean Allman Gilmore
Irene Taurins

From the RC-AAM listserv:

Hello Registrars,

How does one accurately figure shipping/crating costs for a touring exhibition that is three or more years down the road? I have been asked to determine the shipping/crating costs for unknown exhibition venues with an incomplete (and ever-changing) exhibition checklist. Does anyone know if this can be done and would you share your infinite wisdom with me?

—Desperate in the Deep South

Gentle Registrar:

Use your imagination and experience and become an artist: take all worst cases, make no promises, and give your administration a copy of this book.

CHAPTER 2

Concepts

Exhibitions in museums range from those produced totally in-house using the museum's permanent collections to borrowed traveling exhibitions that come with all components and are installed with little deviance from an original plan. In between, there are exhibitions comprised of both loans and permanent collection objects, exhibitions that are completely borrowed from a number of lenders, and exhibitions done in partnership between two museums, with permanent collections from both or loans making up the final product. The variations seem endless, and each exhibition brings its own unique set of problems, demands, and triumphs.

2-1 DEFINITIONS

Throughout this text, we have called each party involved in the traveling exhibition by a specific name or names so that roles remain clear.

Organizer or organizing institution	The institution that is primary organizer and is legally responsible for the exhibition
Exhibitor, exhibiting institution, venue	The institution that contracts to show an exhibition created by an organizing institution
Lender	The owner of objects who lends them to an organizer for use in a traveling exhibition
Borrower	Because borrower could be construed to be the organizer (for works lent) or the exhibitor (for the exhibition), the word is not used unless the context is clear.

2-2 EXHIBITION AND TOUR CONCEPT

Checklist for the Curator
1. Generate idea for an exhibition.
2. Perform preliminary research.
3. Draw up a wish list of objects.
4. Discuss with director.

5. Present to director or exhibitions committee for approval.

Changing exhibitions form the central programming of most museums, but it is nearly impossible for museums to generate enough exhibitions in-house to fill a continuous schedule. Many museums offer a variety of exhibitions during the year. They have "permanent" galleries that feature collection objects and change slowly over the course of several years; they may only be completely reinstalled as part of a major review of collections or a change of direction of the institution. Most museums also have small exhibitions that change fairly often and galleries that may be dedicated to local subjects or artists, to curriculum in a university museum, to new acquisitions, or to a local or national event of significance.

The most visible exhibitions, the ones that are most highly marketed, are large temporary exhibitions. They can bring vitality to a museum, encourage repeat visits from community members, and provide a way to reach new audiences. Temporary exhibitions can be produced in-house and be shown only once, they can be expanded for travel to several venues, or they can be borrowed from another institution or exhibition service that has produced them for travel.

Traveling exhibitions can have great scholarly value and be exquisitely designed; they can reach great numbers of visitors and plot new territory for the museum. Or they can fall flat. The value and eventual success or failure lie in the concept, the integrity of the objects chosen, and the versatility of the design. Careful and continuous oversight of all exhibition details and communication among those producing the exhibition and between the organizing institution and the exhibiting institutions are essential to successful, effective traveling exhibitions.

2-3 TRAVEL

Traveling exhibitions can be produced in collaboration with a traveling exhibition service, such as the

Smithsonian Institution Traveling Exhibition Service (SITES), or they can be organized and circulated by a single museum. This book is geared toward the museum that wants to circulate one or more exhibitions on its own and does not have a specialized department to care for this aspect of its program. Our aim is to help the collections staff who work with the objects and shape them into an exhibition that can withstand the rigors of the road. Our focus is on the registrar, curator, traveling exhibitions coordinator, exhibition designer, and preparator and the ways in which they manage an exhibition. These staff members remain most actively involved in the exhibition while it travels.

The decision to circulate an exhibition should be considered carefully to be certain the museum should take on this task. The visibility and reputation of the museum will increase, the audiences reached will expand tremendously, and there is even a chance, though it is a slight one, that the tour will produce enough revenue to help offset the production costs of the original exhibition. Revenue must, at a minimum, equal the costs of travel; otherwise, the exhibition will be a drain on the institution's budget. Whether there is revenue beyond the cost for travel depends on the pricing, ability to book all slots for the exhibition, and the efficiency of the staff in producing and maintaining the exhibition. A traveling exhibition demands a large commitment of staff time and that cost should be taken into account along with the billable costs of the exhibition.

To ensure that the project proceeds with the least amount of difficulty, the decision to circulate an exhibition must be made during the early planning stages. A museum likely will have a group in place that works together on the exhibitions that it produces (or borrows) and installs. As soon as the exhibition's concept is officially approved by the director or exhibitions committee and work begins on its organization, the group should begin discussions about sending the exhibition on tour. The checklist might change drastically if travel is the goal: light-sensitive objects will require backups, and conservation reviews will determine what is too fragile to travel. Lenders will be asked to lend for longer time periods and be informed that there will be multiple venues. Large and bulky or fragile objects may be used only at the first venue and then replaced for the tour by objects that can withstand travel and frequent handling.

Exhibition design is also dramatically influenced by the need to travel. If there are architectural elements in the exhibition, they should disassemble into small pieces that can be put together and taken apart easily without benefit of the original architect. Planners must keep in mind the sizes of facilities at borrowing venues to avoid an unhappy confluence of large crates and small or difficult loading docks and elevators. Solutions to installation problems must be universal and not specific to the configuration of the original site; careful drawings and photographs of installation specifics are required.

Organizers must produce a design book to guide exhibitors through their own installation of the exhibition. Decisions must be made about whether mounts are for one-time use or if they will travel with the exhibition as well. Marketing and educational packets for the traveling exhibition have to be created, too. There is definitely much more work involved than there is for the single-site exhibition, and the museum administration must be aware of and make allowance for the extra burden that all staff will be expected to bear.

A well-organized traveling exhibition program, should a museum want to include one, takes several years to put in place. Because exhibitions are produced by the museum's staff, they can be slotted into the traveling exhibition program time line. Institutions that have staff dedicated to traveling exhibition programs sometimes do market research long before they begin work on the exhibitions. The Cincinnati Museum of Natural History, for example, created an "Exhibit Topic Survey for Museum Colleagues" to judge in advance the popularity and marketing potential of exhibitions on a variety of topics.

If it is to be successful and give the museum administration the payback it desires, the single or casual traveling exhibition must be put together with as much care as one that is part of an organized program.

2-4 DRAMATIS PERSONAE

Traveling exhibitions are the product of a large cast of characters. They usually start, as do other exhibitions, with the strength of a collection, a curator's idea, and a director's enthusiasm for that idea. As decisions are made, colleagues, consultants, and vendors become involved. As noted previously, plans for travel should come early and help determine checklists, design, materials, marketing, and education. By the time an exhibition hits the road, it will have touched almost everyone in the organizing museum and a number of people in other institutions. The list that follows notes the *roles*, and not necessarily the actual personnel, who will be involved in the exhibition. Use it to fill in personnel in the museum and others outside the museum, as the necessary jobs are assigned. In many cases, one person will take on two (or more) roles.

Someone must play each of these roles. Not every institution has a coordinator of traveling exhibitions or a public relations (PR) officer or a mount maker, but the roles *must* be filled by a staff member or by a consultant, contractor, or vendor

Exhibition staff	as played by	Organizing museum staff
Director		_____
Curator		_____
Coordinator of exhibitions		_____
Coordinator of traveling exhibitions		_____
Development officer		_____
Grants writer		_____
Marketing officer		_____
Public relations officer		_____
Registrar		_____
Traveling exhibition registrar		_____
Courier		_____
Database manager		_____
Conservator		_____
Exhibition designer		_____
Graphic design and production		_____
Preparator		_____
Mount maker		_____
Display furniture producer		_____
Installation technician		_____
Crate maker		_____
Packer		_____
Shipper		_____
Photographer		_____
Editor		_____
Publisher		_____
Insurer		_____

Additional Roles Specifically for the Exhibition Tour:

Director	may attend important openings
Curator	may travel for openings, public lectures, docent education, or courier in some situations
Registrar	serves as primary courier of the exhibition
Preparator	steps in when installations are particularly complex or difficult
Conservator	may travel to each venue to complete condition checks for fragile objects or remain on call, in case needed

2-5 MARKETING THE EXHIBITION

Checklist for Marketing
1. Gather all basic information about the exhibition.
2. Decide on marketing areas.
3. Produce a marketing packet.
4. Contact potential exhibitors (the "A" list).
5. Follow up on any queries.
6. Make initial bookings.
7. Begin drawing up contracts.
8. Contact potential exhibitors (the "B" list).

Marketing occurs in many forms: catalogs published by exhibition touring companies; personal contacts by curators, directors, and other museum personnel; advertisements at museum conferences and in museum publications; and announcements mailed to museums that are carefully chosen for their geographic placement or collection strengths.

The exhibition that is carefully constructed, that has excellent scholarship, an imaginative interpretation, interesting graphics, and great objects will be the easiest to market. The exhibition must also, if possible, provide information on a topic of current interest or be groundbreaking in a particular field. Midsized and small museums are not expected to produce and circulate blockbusters; the exhibitions they do, however, can be of exceptional scholarship and interest.

The museum must designate a coordinator of traveling exhibitions. This person will be responsible for marketing the exhibition and will do what is needed to book the tour venues, including putting together a packet that can be sent to potential venues. The curator produces a checklist for the packet (details to come) and writes a brief overview of the exhibition, stressing its depth and importance to the field. The curator also works with the museum's photo archivist or a photographer to make available images of the most important objects in the checklist.

The marketing packet should contain the checklist; a series of digital images or photographs; the exhibition overview; a catalog, if one has been produced; press cuttings, if they are available; and, most important, a cover page that outlines essential information:

- Title of exhibition
- Organizing exhibitor with contact name and address, telephone, cell, and e-mail
- Loan period dates, exhibition opening date, and exhibition closing date
- Participation fee, with a note that details what the fee covers
- Shipping type and shipping fee
- Contents of exhibition
- Size in square feet or running feet
- Insurance requirements
- Credit lines

The exhibition packet also can be sent, at least in part, electronically. As technology has improved, much of the marketing can be done by e-mail, and available exhibitions can be advertised on the museum's website.

The coordinator of exhibitions and the curator will discuss possible venues, choosing them according to size and ability to pay the tour fee and meet the exhibition standards. They will take into consideration potential interest in the exhibition's subject, based on the potential venue's local community, collections, and geographical region. An "A" list should be determined, and packets should be sent to every museum on that list, with personal follow-up by the coordinator of exhibitions and the curator until the targeted museums decide whether to book the exhibition.

Remember that exhibitions must be marketed at least two years before they are to be sent on the road. Museums may finalize their exhibition schedules two to five years in advance, so traveling exhibitions must be planned even earlier.

CHAPTER 3

Creating the Exhibition

3-1 THE CHECKLIST

A complete checklist forms the core of a successful exhibition. "Complete" means that the checklist contains the actual works that will be in the exhibition and that the information about those works and objects is comprehensive and correct. The earlier the list is complete, and the less it changes, the easier it will be to assess, market, prepare, and travel the exhibition.

Checklist for the Curator*

1. Determine which permanent collection objects will be in the exhibition.
2. Produce label information for checklist.
3. Forward list to registrar and conservator for review.

If loans are included in the exhibition:

4. Determine loans to be requested, if any.
5. If not familiar with objects to be borrowed, visit lending institution.

6. Write letters (often signed by the director) requesting loans.

*All administrative reviews, as required by the institution, should be followed during the process of creating the exhibition.

Checklist for the Registrar

1. After receiving permanent collection list, check information for correct facts and credit lines.
2. Determine object's use and projected use.
3. Schedule conservation reviews for objects.

If loans are included in the exhibition:

4. Obtain completed *General Facility Report* (available from the American Alliance of Museums) from exhibiting venues.
5. Send *General Facility Report* from organizer and confirmed venues to potential lenders.

Traveling Exhibition Checklist

The Sampler Museum

A checklist should contain label information about each piece in the exhibition. In addition, it should contain precise measurements and, if known, credit line and insurance value. It should contain the lender's name and basic geographic information, as well. For example, the following pieces will be in the exhibition, *Sample the Future*:

1. Pendant, *Future*, ca. 1912
   Tiffany and Company, Newark, New Jersey
   Diamond and silver, 1¾ × ½ in.
   The Sampler Museum
   Gift of Susan F. Middleton, 1934
   34.56
   $56,000
   Any Town, Any State
2. Edgar Westcott, American, 1856–1913
   Bear Mountain, 1898
   Oil on canvas, 16 × 28 in., unframed
   20 × 32 in., framed
   Lent by the Holly Museum

   Gift of Daniel Sinclair, 1999
   1999.1.2
   $500,000
   Lebanon, Conn.
3. John Johansen, American, b. 1968
   Bear Mountain in Space, 2001
   Mixed media, 16 × 12 × 8 in.
   The Sampler Museum
   Purchase 2001, The Stanley Silver Fund
   2001.26.3
   $40,000
   Any Town, Any State

6. Obtain signed loan agreements from lenders.
7. Gather information about loan, crating, shipping, and conservation fees from each lender.

Checklist for the Conservator
1. Review all permanent collection objects for ability to travel.
2. Confer with curator and registrar regarding results.
3. Begin recording notes on object care and restrictions.

Although the creation of the checklist is usually slow and changes over time, it is important to get a firm checklist as early as possible. The curator is usually responsible for establishing, fine-tuning, maintaining, and distributing the master checklist. An assistant curator, the registrar, or the manager of the traveling exhibition may be designated to keep the checklist up to date during the exhibition's tour.

3-2 PERSONNEL AND TIME LINE
The process of creating an exhibition depends, to a large degree, on the structure of the museum and the communication among the various staff members involved. It is important to know the strong points and weak points of an organization. Each position, whether it be curator, registrar, exhibition project director, or manager, has set roles and tasks. These tasks differ from institution to institution, so the various requirements of creating and managing a traveling exhibition must be assigned in the context of an institution's ordinary operating structure: initiation of the exhibition, financial development of grants and sponsorships, documentation, legal contracts with lenders and other institutions, design, packing and shipping, insurance and inventory, and education. A museum without a standing committee to deal with exhibitions should form one that includes representation from each department with responsibilities in the project. It is important that all staff involved have a platform from which to ask questions and to report on work done and work still needed. Such a committee is the place to check on progress toward deadlines and to introduce ideas, regardless of an individual's standing in the institution's hierarchy.

Museums have created many types of exhibition time lines for the production of both in-house and traveling exhibitions. Given the wide range of intellectual and practical involvement needed to produce exhibitions, it is best that establishment of the time line be a group project. A lead who is organized and congenial and has a grasp of all facets of the exhibition can produce a draft of the possibilities for group

discussion. For time lines to work, everyone must buy in to the general plan, and the plan must remain somewhat flexible to accommodate the changes that will inevitably come up until the opening of the exhibition. Including a publication only increases time line complexity.

Time lines should include, at the least, dates on which preliminary and final checklists are due, deadlines for negotiating and securing loans, dates to obtain photography for publicity and publication, and due dates for label copy, design approval, collection of loans, hard opening and closing dates, reception and preview dates, selection of and contracts with tour venues, and finalization of the travel schedule. Seeking bids from and selection of vendors and subcontractors must be included in the time line as well. The list of target dates could grow into the hundreds, so it must be clear and concise. Dates must be reasonable and achievable, but adding elements such as application for US Indemnity, which has only two application deadlines per year, can move target dates much earlier than might initially seem preferable.

3-3 DATABASE FORMULATION
The manual system for organizing an exhibition's data usually consists of a card file, a spreadsheet, or typed and retyped lists. The same information is needed for a traveling exhibition, but here there are other options for organizing that information. The major collections management software packages incorporate features that can be enlisted to track exhibition data, or a simple database can be created using any of several commercially available products.

The most versatile way to track a complicated and fast-changing traveling exhibition is through a database, with accompanying reports that present the information in the appropriate format at various times. If using a database is not an option, a computerized spreadsheet or a table in a word-processing document may expedite the process. To create a database, think first about the reports that will be needed during the exhibition's run. The list of reports that follows may be enlarged, depending on need, as the exhibition progresses.

Traveling Exhibition Reports
Objects
    by artist or culture
    by type/category
    by material/medium
    with restrictions and exhibition notes
    for each venue

Courier information
    lenders requesting couriers
    courier list, with arrival dates, per venue
Lenders
    in alphabetical order
    by geographic location
    with shipping information
Crate lists with full object lists, dimensions, weight, notes

A relational database enables the entry of discrete information once, and then the information can be combined into a variety of desired reports. The following six tables and data fields will produce the aforementioned reports and many others. Because the data fields are organized as tables, they also can be used as the basis for spreadsheets or cards.

The first four tables are object specific and are used to bring the exhibition to the first venue, disperse it from the last venue, and produce reports for use at venues along the way. Database table 5 lists crates and objects as they will travel, and database table 6 tracks information about shipping the exhibition between venues. Producing crate lists and tracking shipping between venues are the most straightforward parts of the process; if time limits the database use, information in those two areas can most easily be tracked manually.

Database Table 1: Objects	
Objects	*Information in the Field*
Object ID	Accession or owner's number
Object Exhibition Number	Assigned for tracking
Object Catalog Number	If a catalog exists for the exhibition
Crate Number [*linked to Table 5: Crates*]	Crate the object will travel in
Object Name	Simple and descriptive term
Lender Name [*linked to Table 2: Lenders*]	
Object Title	For works of art
Object Date	Date object made
Artist or Culture	
Materials/Medium	

Dimensions without mount or frame	
Dimensions with mount or frame	
Credit Line	From loan agreement with lender
Insurance Value	As necessary
Photography Restrictions	
Shipping Requirement [*linked to Table 2: Lenders*]	
Installation Note	
Security Requirements	
RH and Light Levels	
Conservation Note	
Courier [*linked to Table 3: Couriers*]	
Other Restrictions	
Initial Arrival Date	
Venue 1	Yes/No [*whether object travels to this venue*]
Venue 2	Yes/No
Venue 3	Yes/No
Venue 4	Yes/No
Dispersal Date	

Database Table 2: Lenders	
Lender Name	
Contact Last Name	
Contact First Name	
Contact Title	
Address	
City	
State	
Zip	
Country	
Phone	
Alternate Phone	

Mobile	
E-mail	
Loan Form Sent	Date
Loan Form Returned	Date
Lender form necessary	Yes/No
Insurance Value Total	
[drawn from Table 1: Objects]	All objects from one lender
Insured by	Choices are organizer policy, lender policy, exhibition policy, US Indemnity, foreign indemnity
Loan Fee	
Preparation Fee	
Conservation Fee	
Packing/Crating Fee	
Total Fees	Sum of the four fields of fees
Shipping Requirement	
Shipping Firm	
Shipping Contact Name	
Shipping Phone Number	
Shipping E-mail	
Initial Shipment Date	
Courier Requirement	
Date Received	

Database Table 3: Couriers (from Table 2: Lenders)	
Lender	
Courier Last Name	
Courier First Name	
Title	
Phone	
Mobile	
E-mail	
Venue 1	Yes/No [Is courier required?]
Venue 1 Arrival Date	Date

Venue 1 Installation Appointment	Date/Time
Venue 1 Transportation Arranged	
Venue 1 Hotel Name	
Venue 1 Hotel Dates	
Venue 1 Hotel Confirmation #	
Venue 1 Per Diem Total	Currency
Venue 1 Information Sheet Sent	Date
Venue 2 (with expanded fields as for Venue 1)	
Venue 3 (with expanded fields as for Venue 1)	
Venue 4 (with expanded fields as for Venue 1)	

Database Table 4: Exhibitor/Venue	
Venue Name	
Address	
City	
State	
Zip	
Country	
Contact Last Name	
Contact First Name	
Contact Title	
Contact Phone	
Contact Mobile	
Contact E-mail	
Facility Report Received	
Facility Report Approved	
Contract Sent	
Contract Returned	
First Invoice Sent	
First Payment Received	
Second Invoice Sent	
Second Payment Received	
Shipping Invoice Sent	

Shipping Payment Received
Arrival Date, Estimated
Arrival Date, Actual
Arrival Courier Notes
Unpack/Install Dates
Departure Courier Notes
Deinstall/Pack Dates
Departure Date, Estimated
Departure Date, Actual
Notes

Database Table 5: Crates	
Crate #	Assigned for exhibition
Crate Length	
Crate Width	
Crate Height	
Crate Weight	
Packing Notes	
Object #1 [all objects linked in Table 1: Objects]	List of objects in crate
Object #2	
Object #3	
Object #4	
Object #5	
Object #6	
Object #7	
Object #8	
Object #9	
Object #10	
Object # ad infinitum	

Database Table 6: Shipments between Venues
An alternative to this table is to use a simple spreadsheet or word-processing program. The single shipper is chosen after the request for proposal (RFP) process is complete and estimates are in.
Shipper
Shipper Contact
Phone
Mobile
E-mail
Shipment date arrive Venue 1
Venue 1 (linked to Table 3: Couriers)
Contact
Phone
Mobile
E-mail
Shipment date leave Venue 1
Shipment date arrive Venue 2
Venue 2
Contact
Phone
Mobile
E-mail
Shipment date leave Venue 2
Shipment date arrive Venue 3
Venue 3
Contact
Phone
Mobile
E-mail
Shipment date leave Venue3*
Shipment date arrive organizer*

Use if dispersal is from organizer, not from last venue.

Lenders with Object List by Geographical Distribution (for Shipping Arrangements)

City, State	Lender	Object	Shipping Requirements	Courier Requirement
Lebanon, Conn.	Holly Museum	Edgar Westcott, American, 1856–1913 *Bear Mountain*, 1898 Oil on canvas, 16 × 28 in.	Truck, exclusive use	Yes
New York, NY	Meredith Smith	Meredith Smith, American, b. 1937 *Countryside*, 1987 Quilt, cotton and polyester, 84 × 96 in.	Truck	No
New York, NY	New York Museum	Jonathan Small, American, b. 1955 *Taking the Lead*, 1984 Oil on canvas, 80 × 26 in.	Truck	No

Restrictions for Object Display (for Exhibitions Design Department, Security, and Registrar)

Lender	Object	Photography Restrictions	Security Requirement	RH and Light Levels	Courier	Other Restrictions
Holly Museum	Edgar Westcott *Bear Mountain*, 1898 Oil on canvas, 16 × 28 in.	For publicity only	Guard in building 24 hours	50% RH, 15 foot-candles max	Yes	Microenvironment case must be built; use for all venues
Meredith Smith	Meredith Smith *Countryside*, 1987 Quilt, cotton and polyester, 84 × 96 in.	None		5–8 foot-candles max	No	
New York Museum	Jonathan Small, American, b. 1955 *Taking the Lead*, 1984 Oil on canvas, 80 × 26 in.	No photography allowed	Alarm on painting must be provided			

3-4 BUDGETS

Budgets Checklists

The exhibition manager must gather estimates of anticipated costs from all staff members who will incur expenses in producing an exhibition, whether it is in-house or traveling. A checklist of typical expenditures in each area will help staff members make organized and thorough estimates for both the core budget and the travel budget. Typically, personnel in the following areas will be polled for budget data:

Curatorial
Exhibition
Marketing
Registration
Conservation
Education

Some of these persons may be on staff, and others may be hired as consultants or contract workers for the period of time needed.

Core Budgets

Funding for exhibitions may come from the general budget, but it is often attached to grants and sponsorships as well. The responsibilities for grant writing generally fall to curators, registrars, and development personnel. Traveling exhibition income from participation fees adds to the complexity and is often managed separately. Base funding for the exhibitions, plus responsibility for management of the budget for both the in-house exhibition and the traveling components, should be assigned to responsible parties and clearly understandable to all team members.

EXHIBITION COSTS CHECKLISTS BY DEPARTMENT The following list includes possible costs. Some costs may not be incurred; for example, if a catalog is not produced, those fees would not be included.

1. Curatorial
Professional fees
Consultants
Travel

Research
Photography
Catalog design/permissions/publication
2. Exhibition
   Design
   Cases and furniture
   Electrical and lighting
   Mount making
   Labels and panels
   Demolition and construction
   Painting
   Installation
   Part-time personnel
3. Marketing and External Affairs
   Poster and invitation design
   Printing and distribution
   Publicity
   Receptions and programs
   Product development (shop)
4. Registration
   Loan fees
   Preparation/framing/mounting by lenders
   Couriers
   Condition reports before shipment
   Conservation before shipment
   Travel mount
   Packing/crating
   Shipping
   Storage
   Insurance
   Photography and documentation
   Part-time personnel
5. Conservation
   Consultation
   Review of objects
   Sensitive mounting
   Object repair and stabilization
6. Education
   Program development
   Packets and materials
   Photography
   Audio/video/digital accompaniments

Core Budgets Affected by Travel
A traveling exhibition's core budget has the same budget items as a one-time exhibition, but there are areas in which travel may cause changes.

Employee expenses
Employee travel
Loan fees*

Crating of loans and objects from organizing museum's collection*
Shipping, including gathering, inter-venue shipping, and dispersal*
Courier travel, accommodation, and per diem*
Storage*
Insurance costs*
Conservation fees*
Consultants' fees
Part-time personnel, as needed
Installation/deinstallation

*These areas might require an additional amount when an exhibition travels. Loan fees might be larger, with costs added for each additional venue. Crating may be upgraded to withstand multiple-use traveling. Couriers may be requested between venues as well as at the beginning and end of the exhibition. Conservators may need to be on call for emergency repairs or object examination at participating venues. Several loans may be crated together for the traveling portion of the exhibition, with, perhaps, local soft pack and transportation available for consolidation (i.e., combining loans from disparate geographical areas so that they can be shipped as a unit to minimize costs, rationalize crating, and simplify shipping schedules.)

Exhibition Travel Budgets
EXHIBITION TRAVEL COSTS CHECKLIST BY DEPARTMENT
1. Curatorial
   Staff travel
2. Exhibition
   Labels and panels, design and production, unless shared electronically
   Design guide preparation
3. Marketing and External Affairs
   Promotional packets to book the exhibition
   Press/publicity packets
4. Registration
   Crating
   Shipping
   Insurance
   Condition book production
   Installation instructions, as necessary
   Courier(s)
5. Conservation
   Consultation
   Time and materials for stabilization
6. Education
   Packets and materials

Speakers/trainers
Staff travel

Realistic budgets for exhibition travel can be determined once valid information is available about an exhibition. In addition to the "final" checklist, the duration of the exhibition and the venues' locations become important issues.

For simpler shows without loans or with only a few loans from other lenders, almost all of these items, except shipping, can be worked into the exhibition fee. Some organizers will include a courier to accompany the exhibition at each transit, whereas others will make the exhibitors responsible for all courier expenses. As exhibition preparation progresses, a great deal of staff time will be consumed during parts of the process. Whether or not staff time becomes part of the overall fee is up to the individual institution; a realistic accounting of staff time, however, probably would make the exhibition fee overwhelming.

Budgets always should be estimated on the high side, and it is usual to add about 10 percent a year for unanticipated costs that will be incurred in the future (e.g., special crates for dispersal, shipping cost increases two or three years into the exhibition, etc.).

3-5 RISK MANAGEMENT

Because artifacts and works of art are at greater risk when they travel, precautions taken to protect them must be intensified. The process begins with evaluating the objects. It is important to provide detailed guidelines for handling and installation, and before finalizing contracts, the organizing institution must scrutinize facility reports of exhibiting venues to ensure that their environments and procedures meet object requirements. Security guidelines must be defined, and crating and shipping (see chapter 5) must be carefully controlled. All of these measures are meant to prevent loss. In case there is loss, however, there must be insurance.

With the increasing importance and awareness of national patrimony and repatriation issues, as well as stringent laws governing the movement of specific plants and animals, a legal review of the objects must be part of the object selection process. The US government offers immunity from seizure, which is particularly important in cases of potential ownership disputes.

Facility Reports
Organizers must learn many specific details about the facilities of exhibiting institutions to be certain

of adequate protection of the exhibition and to avoid surprises regarding transport and installation. In the 1970s a task force of the Registrars Committee of the American Association of Museums (now known as the Collections Stewardship Professional Network of the American Alliance of Museums [CSAAM) devised a standard questionnaire about facilities that has been updated through the years. The *General Facility Report*, which is the third edition of the original *Standard Facility Report*, is published by and available from the American Alliance of Museums (AAM). The report standardizes the way information about a facility is reported; it covers all aspects of the facility, from heating, ventilation, and air conditioning (HVAC) to security and fire systems, to types and levels of light and storage area/loading dock configurations. In addition, it asks about personnel for security, installation, and handling.

The organizing institution must request a facility report from each exhibiting venue and review it carefully. The report helps the organizer think about potential problems and work with the exhibitor to devise possible solutions. If, for example, there is natural light in a gallery that cannot be tolerated by objects in the exhibition, the organizer and exhibitor will discuss ways to block the light or otherwise provide protection. In addition to approving the exhibitor's facility, the organizer also must send all relevant facility reports to lenders to the exhibition. Each lender may have questions and must ultimately approve or disapprove having a loan shown at a particular venue.

Immunity from Seizure
Public Law 89-259, *Exemption from Judicial Seizure of Cultural Objects Imported for Temporary Exhibition*, is "an act to render immune from seizure under judicial process certain objects of cultural significance imported into the United States for temporary display or exhibition." It is prudent to review provenance information on all objects from foreign lenders that are being borrowed for a traveling exhibition, but it is often impossible to tell if a specific object may have been stolen or looted at some time in its history. To guarantee that imported objects will not be confiscated by authorities because of a title dispute, the organizer should apply for immunity from seizure for vulnerable objects.

The application requires thorough documentation, including, among other things, a schedule of imported objects, providing descriptions and values; copies of loan, exhibition, and commercial agreements; and lists of places and dates of the exhibition. The application process requires long lead time and should only be started through the US Department of State after the details of the exhibition are in place.

Insurance and Indemnity
Objects and works of art in a traveling exhibition must be insured. Because transport and exhibition involve a great deal of risk to objects, a major concern for the organizer's registrar is the procurement of standard fine arts (collections) insurance, that is, a policy that covers damage to and loss of objects and works of art. Exhibition materials also may be covered, depending on the policy. It is typical for the organizer to procure and maintain insurance, and there are several ways that can be done. Other risks, such as liability and vehicular insurance, are primarily the responsibility of each exhibitor and the shipping company.

The exhibition may be covered by the organizing institution's existing fine arts (collections) insurance policy, a rider or endorsement made to the main policy, or a special fine arts exhibition policy purchased to cover the objects and works of art during the exhibition period. In some cases, an institution may be eligible to apply for US Indemnity (see section). Some lenders may choose to maintain their own insurance and charge the organizer a premium for the duration of the exhibition. The registrar must track all of these insurance arrangements.

In rare cases, the organizer asks the exhibitors to maintain insurance. This is not preferred because insurance policies of various exhibitors may differ, and the organizer must be certain that adequate coverage exists under each policy. As the borrower of record of the individual objects in the exhibition, the organizer is the legally responsible party and must ensure that its obligations to lenders are met. Decisions also must be made about who pays the cost of transit coverage; venues may want to cover the exhibition only while it is on their premises. If venues are asked to cover travel, each travel segment must be a clearly defined responsibility. In the end, it is much simpler and safer for the organizer to insure the entire exhibition.

Primary Fine Arts Insurance
Most museums carry a fine arts (collections) insurance policy that is meant to cover, primarily, the museum's permanent collection and loans. It covers the collection on premises, off premises, and in transit. It covers borrowed objects wall-to-wall, that is, from the moment that an object or artwork is removed from the

owner's custody until that object is returned to and accepted as unharmed by the owner. The coverage is for a value agreed on by the borrower and lender, and not to exceed current market value for the object. If the loan agreement does not include an agreed-on value, an appraisal of the object at the time of the loss will determine the amount of insurance that can be claimed.

Museums usually are unable to insure their collections for total value; few can afford to cover hundreds of millions of dollars' worth of art and artifacts. Instead, they often determine the amount of insurance to buy by finding probable maximum loss (PML), which is a prudent calculation of greatest loss that might occur in one noncatastrophic incident. PML is found by assessing a collection and facility and finding the area in which a single incident will cause the greatest amount of damage. For example, a museum's main gallery contains ten paintings worth $15 million, and the two adjoining galleries contain the museum's most valuable objects, worth another $10 million. These three galleries are in the same HVAC and fire zone, so if a fire hits that area of the building, the loss could be $25 million, assuming that rapid fire response will save the rest of the building. Even though there are millions of dollars' worth of objects in other areas of the museum, the maximum probable loss is around $25 million. The prudent risk manager considers the worst possible disaster in the area of most value and buys insurance to cover that loss.

In this example, then, the target insurance policy is $25 million. The standard fine arts insurance policy will cover transit as well as works at locations other than the property of the owner. Transit limits should be negotiated separately; the limit is per incident, so it limits the value of the work(s) that can travel in any one vehicle. There may be three trucks on the road at one time, each holding the maximum transit limit in value.

Transit limits may be $2 million, $5 million, or more, and they also may incur an additional premium cost. In the past it was usual for insurance companies to charge extra for insuring works in international transit, while including domestic travel in the overall premium cost. Since the early 2000s, however, domestic travel also has become subject to additional premiums. Worldwide transit limits are most often 25 percent of the premises coverage with only a few restrictions. The insurance market fluctuates, and during a soft market period, policies are more comprehensive at lower cost than they are when times are difficult. There may be coverage, for example, to make up for deductibles in indemnification agreements, and overseas transport may not be charged separately. Acts of terrorism were inclusively covered before the September 11, 2001, attack on the World Trade Center in New York; since then, coverage for acts of terrorism remains available but is often at extra cost. Most museums require such coverage for loans from their institution.

As the market tightens and clauses are dropped, it costs more to insure an exhibition. As the market softens, more coverage becomes available. It is always best to discuss all aspects of any policy with the covering insurance representative to ensure that all risks are covered and any assumptions made about coverage are correct.

Museums may use their primary fine arts insurance policy to cover a traveling exhibition. The standard fine arts policy includes the permanent collection as well as objects and works of art on loan to the insured, as noted previously, covering those objects both at the location of the insured and at other locations. As such, it is possible to use the museum's main policy to insure a traveling exhibition, but a careful review should be made before deciding to take this route. If the organizer uses its primary policy and suffers a loss, the renewal rate for that policy may rise; generally, an exhibition-only policy will compensate the loss without affecting the main policy's renewal rates.

To make a prudent decision about whether to use the museum's primary policy, be aware of the clauses and limits of the policy. Ask these questions:

- Is the overall insurance limit high enough to handle the exhibition without difficulty?
- If the primary policy renewal cost may be affected by a loss, is that risk acceptable?
- Are there other loans or permanent collection objects off-site that need coverage and that must be considered before the exhibition objects?
- What are the limits of value for works in transit?
- Will the sites to which the exhibition travels offer the same types of protection as the organizing museum?

The decision must consider overall insurance protection and other loans. Consider this example: The institution's insurance policy is $25 million. The permanent collection is actually worth $75 million, and there are objects valued at $8 million on loan to the museum for other exhibitions. Because loans will be covered first in the event of an incident, the permanent collection actually is insured for only $17 million, if everything is involved in the same catastrophic loss. Now add an exhibition worth $5 million to the mix. Is it wise to reduce the insured amount of the permanent collection even more? The museum's trustees may not be willing to take such a large risk.

Exhibitions of low value or those traveling to only one or two sites may be covered most easily under the museum's main policy. Such coverage might be seen as a cost-cutting measure, but the real risk should be determined before the main collection policy is used. The exhibition may have uncomplicated insurance needs; if so, only one type of insurance may suffice. As the number of loans and the value and fragility of the objects increase, combinations of exhibition insurance, lender's insurance, and indemnification may be needed.

Exhibition Insurance Policies
Many museums cover an exhibition they have organized under their main policy at home, but they are not willing to use that policy to cover the exhibition when it is in transit or at other sites. To avoid claims that would have a negative impact on the institution's primary policy and future premiums, it is common practice to buy a separate policy or rider to cover the exhibition that travels.

Discuss all aspects of the exhibition with the fine arts insurance broker's representative and send information as required. If the organizing museum does not have a broker (e.g., a self-insured government museum), send an RFP to three fine arts insurance companies. The RFP should include a complete checklist with values, the venues of the exhibition, and the dates of the exhibition at each venue.

Standard clauses should include:

- Wall-to-wall (nail-to-nail) coverage
- Coverage of all objects in the exhibition
- Works in transit
- Pairs and sets (value of whole pair or set if part is lost)
- Loss buy back (insured can repurchase if objects are recovered after claim is made)
- Partial loss (cost of restoration and loss of value of piece)

Standard exclusions include:

- Wear and tear
- Gradual deterioration, inherent vice
- Damage resulting from any repairing, restoration, or retouching process
- Shipments by mail (over a stated value)

- War, insurrection, rebellion, civil war, and so forth
- Nuclear reaction or nuclear radiation

A separate review should be made of coverage for earthquake and terrorism.

Insurance companies will make some reasonable demands on the insured, including:

- Materials must be packed and unpacked by competent personnel.
- The insured must do its best to protect the property against loss and damage.
- The insured must keep accurate records of covered property.

Exhibition policies also may include clauses that cover shipping crates. An example from a policy:

Shipping crates are insured for Fire, Theft, and Extended Coverage (e.g., lightning, hail, explosion, riot or civil commotion, vehicle damage, vandalism, and malicious mischief).

Exhibition insurance clearly covers the specific traveling exhibition. Companies and services that deal in traveling exhibitions often use it to ensure that there is no question about whose insurance is primary if a loss occur. Such insurance also is recommended if an exhibition is high in value or more valuable than the coverage offered by the primary insurance policy held by the insuring institution.

Exhibition insurance is clearly a way of balancing risk. With the increased costs of insurance, however, careful review should be made to determine whether to buy special exhibition insurance or fall back on permanent collection policies.

Notes and Definitions

Waiver of subrogation: Exhibiting venues of the traveling exhibition may request waivers of subrogation. Granted by the organizer to the exhibitor, the waiver of subrogation promises that the insurer of the exhibition will not sue the insurer of the exhibitor. The exhibitor's risk is thus diminished. It is not usual for this to occur, but there are some exhibition insurance policies that refer specifically to this process.

Additional insured: The party requesting to be named as additional insured must have a financial interest in the object(s). Therefore, a shipper or organizer cannot be named as additional insured. A waiver of subrogation is the proper wording in this instance, and, of course, it must be approved by the insurer.

Tracking costs: If the exhibition that is touring has several types of insurance, it is essential to keep thorough records and to budget for the costs of various types of insurance. Notes for each lender should detail how the insurance is covered, what the actual costs of that coverage will be, and who will pay the charges. If lenders demand to carry their own insurance and bill the organizer for premiums, such fees definitely should be figured into the budget. As noted previously, the organizer's registrar must track all of the types and costs of insurance.

US Indemnity

The Arts and Artifacts Indemnity program is administered by the National Endowment for the Arts, on behalf of the Federal Council on the Arts and the Humanities, and helps defray exhibition insurance costs. The National Endowment for the Arts website (https://www.arts.gov/artistic-fields/museums) provides the Guidelines and Application Instructions of the Indemnity program:

The Arts and Artifacts Indemnity Act (P.L. 94-158, and as amended, P.L. 110-161, Sec 426) authorizes the Federal Council on the Arts and the Humanities (a coalition of presidentially-appointed Cabinet-level departments and agencies) to make Indemnity agreements with individuals, non-profit, tax-exempt organizations and governmental units, at no cost for the coverage, for international and domestic purposes.

International Indemnity may cover:

1. eligible objects from outside the United States while on exhibition in the U.S.;
2. eligible objects from the United States while on exhibition outside the U.S., when part of an exchange of exhibitions, except in countries with government indemnity programs (only one of the two exchanges may be requested); approval is rare as there must be strong justification to risk the financial interests of the U.S. abroad;
3. eligible objects from the United States while on exhibition in the U.S. if the exhibition includes other eligible objects from outside the U.S., which must be integral to the exhibition as a whole.

There is no minimum object value for loans in the exhibition required for this program. Exhibitions with international components must be certified by the U.S. Department of State as being in the national interest.

Domestic Indemnity may cover:

eligible objects from the United States while on exhibition in the U.S. An exhibition may include objects from outside the U.S. and/or travel to and from the U.S.; however, coverage is limited to U.S.-owned objects while in the U.S.

There is a minimum object value of $75 million for all U.S. loans in the exhibition required for this program.

The full faith and credit of the United States back the Indemnity agreement. In the event of loss or damage to an indemnified object the Federal Council must certify the validity of the claim and request Congress to authorize payment.

Indemnity applications often require a long lead time to prepare detailed information about objects in the exhibition, packing and shipping methods and agents, environmental and security protection, and standards of handling and care. Lender values must be corroborated by independent appraisals to assess their reasonableness, and application deadlines for each program occur only twice a year. Organizations should plan well in advance if indemnity is to be requested.

Most objects from public and private collections are eligible for indemnity against damage and loss. Art works, artifacts and objects, rare documents, books and other printed materials, photographs, films, and electronic materials fall within the scope of coverage. Applications, which are rigorous and thorough in demanding detail and specific information, are reviewed by the Indemnity Advisory Panel (comprised of museum curators, a conservator, and a registrar) for recommendation to the Federal Council, which grants or denies indemnity, either in part or in full.

Once approved, the indemnitee is responsible for the first layer of payment in the event of a validated claim for damage or loss, via an ascending scale of deductibles: the greater the approved amount of indemnity, the higher the deductible. Deductibles and values not covered by indemnity (e.g., objects with ineligible materials, or, value in excess of indemnity awarded) must have separate insurance coverage. Depending on market availability or on the insurance history of the borrower(s), deductible coverage may be carried on the organizer's fine arts policy; or it may be necessary to purchase an endorsement or a separate policy for the deductible. It is vital to read insurance policies carefully and discuss this issue with the exhibition insurer prior to applying for indemnity.

In sum, since its inception in 1975, the indemnity program has supported exhibitions of every size, type, and value, offering the US public the opportunity to see treasures from around the world that they might not otherwise have had the chance to experience.

Indemnity FAQ

Patricia Loiko, indemnity administrator

Terms of Coverage

Does indemnity cover losses from terrorism and natural disasters?

Yes, the Certificate of Indemnity considers losses resulting from terrorism, war, civil commotion, and earthquakes, hurricanes, wildfires, and so forth. Because these causes are included, they are not specifically listed as exclusions.

What are the exclusions?

The coverage is considered all risk, with few exclusions. As stated in the Certificate: "This certificate indemnifies against all risks of physical loss or damage from any external cause except normal wear and tear, inherent vice, or damage sustained due to or resulting from any repairing, restoration or retouching process." Indemnity is in effect from the completion of the first condition report through the completion of the final condition report, unless otherwise approved.

Are certain types of objects excluded from coverage?

Yes, the Federal Council on the Arts and the Humanities (the agency that determines which applicants receive indemnity) has guidelines to explain the programs' risk management policies. Objects that the Federal Council generally excludes because of fragility include oil on copper paintings; frescoes; those containing pastel, charcoal, certain chalk, lacquer, certain types of glass (including enamels), marquetry, on parchment or vellum; and objects exceeding certain dimensions. If an object is determined ineligible from indemnity coverage it must be otherwise insured.

Are there absolute requirements?

Yes, indemnity will not be approved for inaugural exhibitions in new buildings or substantially renovated spaces; couriers must ride on board every conveyance transporting indemnified objects; human presence is mandatory inside buildings where indemnified objects are located (except lender residences) 24/7/365. All other logistics are determined on a case-by-case basis.

Are subcontractors involved with the exhibition, for example, packers, airlines, truckers, and security guards, liable for losses?

No, all of the above, and employees of the organizer and venue museum(s) are waived from subrogation as outlined in the certificate, except if the loss occurs as a result of gross negligence or willful misconduct.

What is the loss buy-back provision?

If an object is recovered after payment has been made, the original owner has the right to repurchase the object from the Federal Council for the amount paid at the time of the loss. If the owner opts not to repurchase, the object will be sold at public auction.

If the lender is a sovereign or the agent of a sovereign (a government-owned museum, for example), the sovereign retains title to the object even after the Federal Council has reimbursed for the loss. If the object is recovered, it is returned to the owner for the amount paid by the Federal Council.

Claims

How are claims paid?

If a claim for loss or damage to an object is certified as valid by the Federal Council, the Federal Council requests payment from Congress. The length of time to process a claim can vary depending upon the circumstances. If a theft has occurred, the Federal Council investigates thoroughly in hope of recovery. If an object is damaged, loss in value cannot be ascertained until after conservation is complete. Claims are reviewed at the meetings of the Federal Council, which occur quarterly each year.

In the event of disagreement about the amount of loss in value or depreciation, the federal regulations governing indemnity outline an arbitration process (45 CFR part 1160.10). In brief, both sides (the lender and the Federal Council) choose an expert to act in their behalf. If the two experts cannot agree on the amount of loss, they select a third party expert, whose opinion is final.

Can claims be paid in a foreign currency?

No, all lender values are reported on the application in US dollars because this is the basis for payment if a claim is made. Indemnity coverage has a congressionally authorized liability limit at any one time, which cannot be exceeded. A validated claim payment would be made to the indemnitee, who in turn would pay the lender; if a lender requires payment in a foreign currency, the indemnitee is responsible for the conversion exchange.

What happens if a foreign currency fluctuates after the application has been submitted?

Most lenders give values of their loans in their currency on the loan forms. The borrower then converts the currency and puts the US dollar amount on the indemnity application. The guidelines allow for rounding up the conversion by a reasonable amount to accommodate any adverse fluctuations expected during the time of indemnity coverage. If the organizer anticipates that a currency will fluctuate greatly over a long tour, for example, it may be necessary to purchase a commercial insurance policy to cover the difference between indemnity and the foreign currency conversion at the time of loss.

APPLICATION PROCESS

When should an application be submitted?

The guidelines advise that applications should not be submitted more than fifteen months in advance of the opening of the exhibition. The application must contain specifics about airline carriers, truckers, venues, couriers, lender values, and so forth, any of which might need to be revised if the lead time before logistics are implemented is too long. The most successful applications have complete information at the deadline; however, applicants must decide which deadlines are best for their projects. Electronic submissions are accepted twice each year: for International Indemnity, on March 15 and September 15; for Domestic Indemnity, on June 15 and December 15.

Are successful applications available for review?

No, for security reasons, previous applications cannot be shared. Applicants might seek help from colleagues who have completed indemnity applications (the website link for each program includes a list of recently indemnified exhibitions). The process is quite different from grantsmanship because the application covers facility, transportation, and object information. It is key that application instructions are carefully reviewed and all requested information is provided (answers may be as long as necessary).

Can private collectors remain anonymous?

No, the names must be revealed to the Federal Council before a Certificate of Indemnity is issued, to be certain that the US Treasury is not put at risk for an owner whose foreign or domestic policy interests may not be the same as the government's. Names can be sent confidentially directly to the Indemnity Administrator's office.

For additional information, contact the Indemnity Administrator at the National Endowment for the Arts.

Terrorism Coverage Update

Rebecca A. Buck

Insurance policies are shaped by times and places. The insurance market, however, is global, and the amount of money invested in the world's insurance pool is finite. When disaster strikes, profits go down, money becomes tight, rates go up, and as happens in the face of terrorism, investors grow nervous and reluctant to insure against the risk responsible for the situation.

Like many other businesses and the economy itself, the insurance industry moves in cycles. When premiums are strong, the market is "hard," and when rates turn low, it is a "soft" market. For much of the 1990s, the insurance market was soft, and there was an abundance of money available to cover risks. Brokers offered low rates, rewards, and incentives to customers shopping for the best insurance products for their money. For museum fine arts (collections) policies, foreign and domestic transit were often offered without additional premiums, coverage was available for deductibles incurred in the indemnification process, and prices were, in general, low. The fact that the museum world has a good record for documenting and protecting its collections and for keeping losses down made insuring museum collections attractive.

Fine arts (collections) policies, which grew from "inland marine" policies used to cover goods in transit on ships, have several standard exclusions. They do not cover wear and tear, gradual deterioration, vermin, inherent vice, shipments by mail or "on deck," war, insurrection, rebellion, revolution, civil war, usurped power, or governmental action against such events; they do not cover nuclear reactions or radiation. Because terrorism had not been in the list of exclusions in standard collections policies, it was covered on September 11, 2001.

Before September 11, terrorism loss was not a major factor in the United States. Covering terrorism in insurance policies under the general premium was actually a good investment for insurance companies. In Europe, where terrorism was experienced from several sources (Irish Republican Army bombers, Basque separatists, the Initial Reaction Force), many countries established terrorism insurance pools, a form of state indemnification. On September 11 everything changed for the United States; in addition to the devastating losses of life and corporate property, an estimated $100 million in public art was lost in the World Trade Center; art was also destroyed in the Pentagon. Added to these losses was the destruction of many artists' studios in New York, as well as corporate and private collections of unknown amounts; one artist-in-residence at the World Trade Center, Michael Richards, died in the attack.

These terrorist attacks, coupled with the economic difficulties that followed, hastened the end of the soft insur-ance market and came close to ending terrorism coverage, as well. The total payout for the losses of September 11 was estimated at $60–$70 billion; AXA Art Insurance Company paid out $17.2 million for the claims from three corporate collections they covered.[1] Although art loss was a minor part of the whole, the pool of money to cover terrorism damages dried up shortly after the events.

There was an immediate impact on museums. The Newark Museum, for instance, was expecting a large shipment of artworks from the Netherlands, accompanied by several couriers, on September 12, 2001. The shipment was part of the exhibition *Art and Home: Dutch Interiors in the Age of Rembrandt*, produced in partnership with the Denver Art Museum. The exhibition was to open on September 25. The opening was delayed several weeks, and works came in slowly, as airlines resumed schedules and couriers regained the courage to travel. Several of the Dutch lenders decided not to accept the insurance coverage that had been agreed on and instead formed a consortium to buy their own policy. Although both policies covered terrorism, there was much confusion, and they felt more comfortable with their own policy. The exhibition opened with two works outstanding, one from England and one from Russia.

The scant amount of terrorism coverage that could be found, if any, was at exorbitant rates. Even without terrorism, insurance rates rose dramatically. Rates for some fine arts policies that were renewed at the end of 2001 doubled and included no terrorism coverage.

The great fear among museums centered on the possibility that loans vital to exhibitions would be denied. To counter this prospect as directly as possible, the Association of Art Museum Directors (AAMD) took early action for their members. On February 9, 2002, they passed the following motion: "Be it resolved that no museum in the Association of Art Museum Directors will require any other AAMD member museum to procure terrorism insurance for the loan of any single work or for exhibitions in their entirety." They based this action on their discussions:

> It was agreed that the cost of this new insurance requirement has, since September 11, become prohibitive, and if required of museums, would effectively prevent the staging of major exhibitions. While a real risk of terrorist attacks on art museums may exist, the committee members felt that the risk was exaggerated in the immediate aftermath of the attack on the World Trade Center last September, and that current rates were therefore excessive.[2]

Although this resolution eased the immediate problem for inter-museum loans originating in the United States, it did not address the larger issues. Terrorism insurance needed to be available again for all property, including museum loans, at less than prohibitive rates, and the most logical way to support that insurance was through government action. A major lobbying consortium was formed, and AAMD signed on as one of the members. It was successful, and in 2002 the Terrorism Risk Insurance Act (TRIA) was passed.

TRIA directed that the Secretary of the Treasury, in concurrence with the Secretary of State and the Attorney General of the United States, be given the power to certify acts of violence as terrorism and to initiate partial insurance coverage by the US government for damage caused by those acts.

TRIA set up a system that shares public and private compensation for insured loss from terrorism. There is a formula for determining how much coverage will be public, that is, from the federal government; and how much will be private, that is, from insurance clients, charged through a "policy surcharge for terrorism loss risk-spreading premiums." Rates for terrorism insurance are determined yearly by the Secretary of the Treasury, and insurance companies have to offer terrorism coverage to clients.

The program had only slight changes until it expired in 2005, at which time the option to renew the act was taken (Terrorism Risk Insurance Extension Act). The law was again updated in 2007 and became the Terrorism Risk Insurance Program Reauthorization Act (TRIPRA). There was a major change in the 2007 version. The original coverage of terrorism directed that, to be certified a covered act of terrorism, the violent act must be committed "by an individual or individuals acting on behalf of any foreign person or foreign interest." In 2007, the phrase regarding foreign involvement was removed, so the program now covers domestic terrorism as well as terrorism acts by foreign actors. The law has undergone other small changes, but in 2015 it was again reauthorized and is set to expire on December 31, 2020.

Policies are now being written in compliance with TRIPRA guidelines: The insurer is directed to notify its clients that they have a right to purchase insurance coverage for losses arising out of certified acts of terrorism. Clients are asked to sign rejections if they do not wish to include the coverage in their policies. It is advisable to know your brokers well and to read offered policies extremely carefully. Some policies covering "terrorism" do not, in fact, cover much at all. In some states, such as New York, it is illegal to restrict fire coverage regardless of cause; thus, in that state, you may not have terrorism coverage but you may be covered, by law, for fires started by terrorist acts. Some insurance companies have decided to rule for themselves that an act is covered terrorism, rather than wait for governmental authorization.

There have been no major terrorism claims since the September 11 incidents, and rates for terrorism coverage are lower in the current soft market. Markets will change again as different environments demand, but there will always be a need for coverage in this world that changed so drastically on September 11. The next chapter of this particular story will be written when TRIPRA expires on December 31, 2020. Continue monitoring legislative activity in Washington to keep up to date.

NOTES

1. Dietrich von Frank, president and CEO of AXA Art Insurance Company, speaking at the International Foundation for Art Research Symposium on the Art Lost on September 11, 2001, said in February 2002: "I have been asked many times how much art was destroyed on September 11th in total, and I have always said, 'I don't know!' We still don't know, and we probably will never know unless accurate record keeping of all perished pieces exists, which I very much doubt. AXA Art's three clients kept accurate records, and checks to the insured will go out soon."
2. AAMD Press Release, February 9, 2002; Laura Chistofferson, administrative assistant.

BIBLIOGRAPHY

Ad Watch: The Battle for Terrorism Insurance. Available at: www .opensecrets.org/alerts/v6/alertv6_55.asp.

Coalition to Insure Against Terrorism. Available at: www.insure againstterrorism.org.

Collins, Michael. "9-11—One Year Later: The disadvantage of being a high-profile place." *Naples Daily News*, Naples, Florida (Scripps Howard News Service), September 11, 2002.

Cuno, James. "A World Changed? Art Museums after September 11." Available at: http://www.amacad.org/publications/bulletin/ summer2002/cuno.pdf, Stated Meeting Report, Summer 2002.

International Foundation for Art Research. "Edited Proceedings: September 11th: Art Loss, Damage, and Repercussions, An IFAR Symposium–February 28, 2002." *IFAR Journal*, Volume 4, Number 4/Volume 5, Number 1, 2001/2002, pp. 8–33. International Foundation for Art Research, New York, New York.

International Foundation for Art Research. "September 11th and the Art World." *IFAR Journal*, Volume 4, Number 3, 2001, pp. 2–3. International Foundation for Art Research, New York, New York.

Pub. L. 107-297 Stat. 2322 (TRIA).

Pub. L. 109-144, 119 Stat. 2660 (TRIEA 2005).

Pub. L. 110-160, 121 Sta. 1839 (TRIPRA 2007).

Pub. L. 114-1, 129 Stat. 3 (TRIPRA 2015).

Resource Center: Terrorism Risk Insurance Program. Available at: www.treasury.gov.

Vogel, Carol. "Fears of Terror a Complication for Art Exhibits." *New York Times*, February 25, 2003.

von Frank, Dietrich. "Response from the Insurance Industry, Edited Proceedings: September 11th: Art Loss, Damage, and Repercussions, An IFAR Symposium–February 28, 2002." *IFAR Journal*, Volume 4, Number 4/Volume 5, Number 1, 2001/2002, pp. 21–22. International Foundation for Art Research, New York, New York.

Weaver, Jane. "Paying terror's premiums." Available at: www .msnbc.com/news/740038.asp, April 29, 2002.

3-6 DETERMINING THE EXHIBITION FEE

In general, museums do not circulate an exhibition to make up the cost of creating and showing the exhibition on their own premises. In distributing the exhibition, the museum first will show off its creativity, skill, and scholarship and spread its name and reputation and only then will it make (or attempt to make) a small profit from the touring portion to feed back into the cost of the original exhibition. The money it garners from exhibition fees often goes toward salary costs of the personnel who manage traveling exhibitions. At the very least, all travel expenses and direct costs for circulating the exhibition must be covered.

The traveling portion of the exhibition, including extraneous expenses (e.g., extra catalogs, staff travel, design and condition books) should be incorporated into the estimate the museum uses to determine the cost of circulating the exhibition. Ideally, estimating all of the costs and dividing by the number of venues will form a basis for the exhibition fee. The fee that is finally charged, beyond these costs, will include a subjectively determined "value" of the exhibition. This is generally a marketing decision based on the cost of similar exhibitions, the intrinsic value of the objects, and the relative popularity of the subject. The travel costs should include:

- all staff travel and expenses;
- staff salaries and benefits determined by time spent on the exhibition;
- preparation and conservation costs;
- initial crating and packing;
- crating, shipping, and packing for replacement works;
- catalogs, if included;
- upkeep of exhibition labels, text, and photograph panels;
- loan fees per exhibition;
- insurance costs;
- storage fees, if necessary;
- production of condition report book;
- preparation of design book; and
- overhead, traditionally determined by the individual institution.

The largest expense for the travel portion of most exhibitions is crating and packing. The eighteen crates needed for *Sample the Future*, for example, may cost $25,000, and another $10,000 will be spent on packing. If there are to be replacement textiles or rotation of works on paper, the crating and shipping of those works, as well as storage of the ones "off" exhibit, should be included. Lenders may charge a loan fee per venue, so loan fees and insurance fees also should be incorporated in the travel expense.

Staff travel costs should include round-trip expenses at the beginning and the end of each exhibition period (if the organizer sends a courier to pack/unpack, check condition, install/deinstall, and accompany the objects in transit), as well as hotel, and a per diem to cover food, local transportation, phone and internet, and minor entertainment charges. Staff salaries include the courier and also the exhibition design staff, mount makers, and registrars who work on parts of the ongoing exhibition. The number of catalogs multiplied by the production cost should be included, as should the design book production (staff and materials) and the condition book preparation (staff, photography, and materials).

Consider this example: Egyptian subjects are popular and can garner a minimum of $40,000 in fees. Analysis of expenses indicates that the exhibition will cost $25,000 per venue, so the fee must be at least $40,000 to make a profit of $15,000. Thus, $40,000–$45,000 would be a good range for the exhibition fee. Although this example makes the exhibition look profitable, the key is to fill all of the bookings and not have to store or dismantle the exhibition during the tour.

The person or department in charge of coordinating the exhibition for the organizer should survey colleagues at potential exhibiting venues to determine levels of interest in the particular exhibition topic and do research to establish the relative value of the exhibition compared to similar offerings. Numerous exhibition services, both commercial and not-for-profit, offer traveling exhibitions; internet research will reveal many examples. Use them to compare and contrast.

A major problem in budgeting and setting fees for traveling exhibitions will be encountered if the checklist is not completed at an early date. The exact works must be used to determine loan consolidation costs and fees, crating configurations and costs, insurance types and amounts, space needs, shipping options, and the exhibition fee itself. If possible, the complete checklist for the exhibition should be included in the marketing packet. Ideally, there should be several years of planning and research, with reliable information available for grant writing, loan decisions, and perhaps, information gleaned from tour marketing. This situation does not always materialize, however, especially at institutions producing a first traveling exhibition.

If it is not possible to have a real and complete checklist to work with (and it rarely is), the next best thing is a mock list that contains as many of the actual works as possible, the probable objects that are being negotiated for, and the rest of the curator's wish list. Because much exhibition planning is done in this mode, it becomes a mix of art and practicality to determine exhibition budgets and fees. The curator, exhibition designer, registrar, and museum administration must rely on their communication skills to keep everyone up to date as the exhibition progresses.

The team concept is essential to the success of the traveling exhibition. Very little information is important to only one or two staff members. Changing or adding one work, for example, may mean a new crate configuration, perhaps a new loan fee, a design change, a catalog addition, a revamped marketing piece, a shipping and insurance change, and an addition to the invitation list for the opening.

The fee for the traveling exhibition is a combination of the work and the cost involved, the costs for the traveling portion, and the market value of the exhibition. A balance must be achieved to sell the exhibition, keep it on the road, and hold it within the realm of museum budgeting.

Exhibition Fee Work Sheet*

The Sampler Museum

Exhibition/Education/Publicity:

Replacement of panels/graphics	$_____
Exhibition design/installation manual	$_____
Education packets	$_____
Publicity packets	$_____
Photography	$_____
Catalogs	$_____

Registrarial:

Loan Fees	$_____
Crating and packing	$_____
Insurance for the entire tour	$_____
Conservation review for travel	$_____
Condition report book	$_____
Courier travel and per diems	$_____
Object replacement/rotation costs	$_____

Administrative:

Consultants	$_____
Postage, telephone, FedEx	$_____

Contingency:

Contingency: storage	$_____
Contingency: damage	$_____
Contingency: frame/crate replacement	$_____

Note: Contingency should amount to 10 to 25 percent on all out-of-pocket costs, if not already built in.

Overhead (Operating budget)	$_____
Total Costs:	$_____

A	Total costs divided by number of venues (__)	$_____
B	+ Reasonable addition to approach current fees for comparable exhibitions	$_____
C	"Profit"	$_____
Fee (A + B + C):		$_____

NOTE: With this method of calculating the fee, the cost of collecting loans from lenders, the transportation of the exhibition from venue to venue, and the return of loans to lenders would be additional costs to be shared among exhibiting venues by some method, to be spelled out.

Figures in this work sheet should be taken from the exhibition travel budget and not the core budget.

CHAPTER 4

Contracts and Contract Negotiations

4-1 CONTRACT PREPARATION

Contract Checklist for Exhibition Organizer
1. Obtain letter of intent in writing (e-mail, fax, or original) from potential exhibitor.
2. Request a completed *General Facilities Report* from borrowing institution.
3. Pencil exhibitor into correct spot on master booking list.
4. Research borrowing institution's legal name.
5. Obtain complete contact information for the borrowing institution.
6. Ask registrar or conservator to review facility report when it arrives.
7. Upon acceptance of *General Facilities Report*, fill in the exhibitor's relevant information in contract (i.e., dates, contacts, fees, etc.).
8. Attach letter, exhibition checklist, booking list, staff list with contact information and request for staff list from exhibitor, and invoice with due date for first payment.
9. Send contract in duplicate.
10. Follow up with phone call to exhibitor, two to three weeks after contract is sent.
11. Answer exhibitor's questions; coordinate negotiations.
12. Follow up with facilities questions and contract negotiations, as necessary.
13. If changes are agreed on, revise and issue a new contract, in duplicate.
14. On receipt of signed contract, countersign and return one copy to exhibitor.
15. Enter exhibitor information into all checklists, databases, and other places that are used to track the exhibition.
16. Note date of payment.

Contracts for traveling exhibitions come in every shape and form imaginable. Language may be clear and basic or formal with legal terminology. As an exhibitor, one may find some contracts "standard" and others so full of specific and special stipulations that each clause merits serious discussion. Simple contracts that leave many questions unanswered and many situations without procedure do not adequately protect any of the parties. On the other hand, contracts that are so complicated they cannot be easily understood create barriers and problems for everyone.

Contracts usually are drawn between the organizer and one exhibitor; and if there are multiple venues, each exhibitor will have a separate contract. There are instances, however, in which an organizer produces one contract and asks all exhibitors to countersign the single document. This is unusual and can be complicated to negotiate.

- There *must* be a contract between exhibitor and organizer for each exhibition.
- The contract *must* be signed by both parties: organizer and exhibitor.
- The contract should lay out all salient points of the exhibition.
- The contract should schedule all fees.
- Rely on the contract and its language whenever a question or dispute arises.

A museum circulating an exhibition should have a clear contract that is easily understandable and covers all areas of the exhibition and its risks completely. In drafting the contract, think of the organizing museum as an exhibiting venue, and ask the questions that an exhibitor would (and definitely will) ask. In all practical areas, however, write the contract to favor the organizing institution.

Ideally, museums that circulate exhibitions should include an attorney review as part of their budget and contract process. If a museum trustee who is an attorney is asked to review a contract, make certain that he or she is familiar with the law of contracts in your state; a criminal lawyer, for example, may not have the needed expertise. Make certain that one person on the staff is designated as the main contact to negotiate the contract. (See the negotiation models later in this chapter.)

Museums that borrow exhibitions should have a clear and concise method for reviewing and negotiating the contract. Although an attorney review is recommended if budget and circumstances allow, museum exhibition contracts have become fairly standard, and staff may decide to consult with counsel only if there are serious questions. All staff involved in the review process, however, should be aware of the various parts of a contract and what is expected in each part and that they may negotiate any or all parts of the contract they receive.

The components of the contract are discussed, and sample contracts are included in the appendixes. Please note that contracts for hands-on exhibitions and exhibitions for nontraditional venues are not covered here; the following contract discussion deals with traditional exhibitions comprised of museum permanent collection and borrowed objects that are shown at other museums.

The Clear Contract

A museum that markets traveling exhibitions might want to prepare a series of standard contracts that can be used for all exhibitions it produces. The Smithsonian Institution Traveling Exhibition Service (SITES), for example, has contracts that cover low-, medium-, and high-risk exhibitions (see item 8, "Facilities"). If the museum does only one type of exhibition (e.g., all low risk), then a single standard contract could be used for all shows. Contract language also can be changed to match situations as they arise.

Cover Page

It is highly recommended that the first page of the contract consist of a cover page. This page should contain all the basic information in a clear and easily accessible format.

Traveling Exhibition Contract

The Sampler Museum

Cover Page

Exhibition title:	*Sample the Future*
Organizer:	The Sampler Museum
Address:	123 Any Street, Any Town, Any State
Contact:	Louise Sample, Exhibition Coordinator
Telephone:	000-000-0001
Mobile:	000-000-0002
E-mail:	lsample@sampler.org
Loan period dates:	October 13, 2020–February 27, 2021
Exhibition public opening date:	November 3, 2020
Exhibition first event:	October 28, 2020
Exhibition closing date:	February 6, 2021
Participation fee:	$25,000
Fee includes:	Exhibition materials (see Appendix A), crating, wall-to-wall insurance, all costs for Sampler courier at installation and deinstallation.

Shipping:	Prorated
Shipping fee:	Not to exceed $7,500
Contents of exhibition:	154 objects, 10 photographs, disc with text panels and label copy, mounts for books only, hanging hardware for framed objects
Other requirements:	Courier oversight for lenders
Fine arts insurance:	Insured by The Sampler Museum
Insurance value:	N/A
Credit:	Sample the Future was organized by The Sampler Museum, Any Town, Any State. The exhibition has received funding from the National Endowment for the Humanities and the New Foundation. Additional support has been received from foundations, corporations, and individuals.

Contract Components

The exhibition's various players and their roles should be clearly known by all parties. The organizing museum may own all of the objects, which certainly makes exhibition risk management simpler. It is rare, however, for this to be the case. The organizing museum usually mixes its own objects with those borrowed from other institutions and individuals and then lends the entire exhibition to a series of borrowing venues. Legal responsibility for the objects rests with the organizer, which signs loan agreements with all of the lenders who have agreed that their objects will travel. (See Appendix E for a sample loan agreement.) In rare instances, lenders will require a separate contract from each borrowing venue; a foreign government, for example, may have contracts with each venue and send a representative to check facilities and a courier to oversee installations. It is usual, however, for communications to be made through the organizing museum.

Several sections in traveling exhibitions contracts ensure that an exhibition will be shown and handled in the way the organizing institution expects. Other clauses explain the specifics of payment, risk management, marketing, and display. Finally, every contract contains several standard clauses that cover various legal situations and protect the organizer's investment in the project.

We discuss the following contract components at some length:

1. Definitions and Agreement to Borrow
2. Fees/Payment Schedule
3. Insurance
   Fine Arts Insurance
   Indemnity
   Immunity from Seizure
4. Exhibition Display/Restrictions
5. Credit Lines/Sponsorships
6. Shipping
   Exhibition Materials
   Couriers
7. Packing/Handling/Care/Condition Reporting
8. Facilities
   Security
   Environment
9. Publicity
   Catalogs
   Promotion
   Photography
10. Damages, Breach of Agreement
11. Notices
12. Successors and Assigns
13. Waivers, Remedies
14. Entire Agreement
15. Attorneys' Fees
16. Severability
17. Governing Law
18. Dispute Resolution
19. Signatures
20. Appendixes

Note: Other clauses may be added, and some requirements may change if an exhibition is deemed to require limited, moderate, or high security; extraordinary environmental controls; or other special requirements.

In the following discussion, we include comments on both the theory and intent of each contract component and on the language that might be used in the agreement itself.

1. DEFINITIONS AND AGREEMENT TO BORROW

Comment The agreement to borrow is absolutely vital to the contract. It contains the basic contractual statements regarding borrowing and lending and all of the relevant information that will guide the organizer and exhibitor through the loan process.

Contract Language

This Agreement is made this December 12, 2019, between The Sampler Museum Trustees, 123 Any Street, Any Town, Any State ("The Sampler Museum" or "Organizer"), and The Bangor Museum, Bangor, Maine ("Exhibitor").

The Sampler Museum has prepared for circulation an exhibition entitled Sample the Future, comprised of objects listed in Appendix A ("the Exhibition"). The Exhibitor desires to display the Exhibition according to the terms and conditions set forth herein.

Exhibitor hereby agrees to borrow and The Sampler Museum agrees to loan the Exhibition for the purpose of exhibition ("loan purpose") on Exhibitor's premises (the "approved location") during the period November 3, 2020–February 6, 2021 (the "exhibition period"); three weeks will be allowed before and after the exhibition period for transportation, unpacking/packing, and installation/deinstallation. Exhibitor agrees to pay in consideration of the loan the amount of $25,000.

Comment Each entity that enters into the contract should be clearly noted and defined in the opening paragraph of the contract, and the date of the contract should be clearly stated:

This agreement is made <<*date*>> by and between <<*institution 1*>> and <<*institution 2*>>.

Learn the legal name of each institution. The Hood Museum of Art, Dartmouth College, is governed by the legal entity *Trustees of Dartmouth College.* The Brandywine River Museum of American Art is governed by *The Brandywine Conservancy & Museum of Art.* Use the legal title in the contract. Sometimes it is important that the department that is entering into the contract be noted (e.g., *Trustees of Dartmouth College through its Hood Museum of Art*).

Defined terms should be placed in quotation marks within parentheses following the definition. The terms will then legally stand in for the longer definition whenever they subsequently appear in the contract.

In the agreement to borrow, identify the exhibition to be borrowed and its exhibition and loan dates. For example, "The Sampler Museum has prepared for circulation an exhibition entitled *Sample the Future,* with objects listed in Appendix A, which the exhibitor desires to display *November 3, 2020–February 6, 2021.*" The borrowing period should be from four to eight weeks beyond the exhibition dates (i.e., an additional two to four weeks at both ends of the exhibition period). This clause also typically explains that the complete object list can be found in the appendix and notes the exhibition's "loan fee" (may also be referred to as "participation fee").

Contract Language

The Exhibition consists of the objects set forth in Appendix A (which is attached and made part of this agreement), object mounts and/or installation hardware, text and other panels and labels (collectively, the "exhibition materials").

Exhibitor will comply with all special instructions of The Sampler Museum as outlined herein and in all written registration notes accompanying the Exhibition with respect to condition, care, handling, installation, presentation, security, and packing of the Exhibition. Care and handling instructions can be found in Appendix B, attached.

Comment Checklists must be accurate and complete, and they must be kept up to date. When rotations are necessary (e.g., paper or textiles objects because of total light exposure allowed, or special stipulations from lenders), they should be noted clearly in the exhibition checklist.

Main Negotiating Points *Dates of exhibition; dates of loan period*: Exhibiting venues often want to make slight adjustments to the exhibition dates. Before the organizer agrees to date changes, it must check the feasibility of shipping from the previous venue or to the next venue. Changes of more than a few days also might affect the exhibition fee.

Contract Standards

Exhibition dates: It is usual to allow three to five weeks between exhibitions, one to two for deinstallation, packing, and travel, and two to three for unpacking and installation. The complexity of the exhibition (i.e., the need for one or more lender couriers, complicated or a large number of mounts, or special installation requirements or assemblies) will dictate the allotment of extra time between showings. Consider the time the organizing museum will need for its own installation and use that as a guide for determining schedules for the other venues.

Labels, mounts, panels: The organizer usually includes label copy (typically in an electronic format) with the exhibition materials. Text panels often are available, as are installation photographs. Display cases rarely travel with the exhibition; they cause the cost of transportation to soar, and unless each case has well-fitted covers and padding, damage to casework is common.

In some instances, the organizing museum may include mounts. Sometimes, as with an installation of large hanging textile, mounts are essential. More often, mounts are dependent on installation design and cases used at each individual venue and, thus, must be provided by the exhibiting institution. The organizer should decide what mounts it can provide for standard installation and ensure that exhibitors are aware of their responsibilities in this area. If the organizer does not supply mounts or installation hardware, there should be discussions regarding standards and requirements for mounts, or the standards may be included in the appendix.

2. FEES/PAYMENT SCHEDULE

Comment Fees for the exhibition should be carefully laid out and accounted for as the exhibition progresses.

The exhibition fee generally includes use of the objects to be exhibited, labels (electronic copy, at the very least), panels or panel information, crates, insurance for the exhibition, care and handling guidelines, condition report books, materials for design and programming, and a limited number of catalogs, if available.

If they are needed for the exhibition, couriers or representatives from the organizing museum, including their transportation, housing, and per diem, are usually part of that cost. Otherwise, the organizing museum should state clearly in the contract that the cost of couriers or representatives is the exhibitor's responsibility. Two types of couriers must be covered: (i) those sent by the organizing institution to oversee shipping or to help with condition reporting and installation/deinstallation and (ii) those required by lenders to the exhibition. Responsibilities for the costs of both types should be clearly delineated in the contract.

Shipping is not usually part of the exhibition fee. Any charges not covered by the exhibition fee should be clearly identified in the contract.

Shipping charges are billed as soon as possible after shipment. Alternatively, the organizer may ask for an estimated shipping fee with the first payment or make the estimated fee due on the date of arrival. Adjustments can be made after all shipping bills are in. In some cases, all shipping billing is done at the end of the tour.

It is prudent to make provision as well for extreme changes in the economy. Insurance, for instance, skyrocketed after the terrorist attacks on September 11, 2001. (See "Terrorism Coverage Update" in chapter 3.) Oil prices and air freight charges, which are sensitive to fluctuations in the economy, can also change drastically. A clause that states that unexpected insurance or shipping increases are to be shared equally helps to protect the organizing institution.

Contract Language

Exhibitor agrees to pay the loan fee to The Sampler Museum in two installments, as follows: (1) $12,500 to be sent with the executed original of the Agreement and (2) $12,500 to be paid by the first day of the exhibition period, or no later than November 3, 2020. The Sampler Museum will provide an invoice to Exhibitor for all payments.

The fee for the exhibition includes use of a fully researched and assembled exhibition with labels, educational materials, publicity packet, and insurance. It also includes catalogs and/or brochures, as noted below. Packing and crating are included. All costs for The Sampler Museum courier, who will help with installation and deinstallation, are included. If lenders require couriers for specific works, the cost of those couriers (transport, lodging, and per diem), will be borne by the Exhibitor. Shipping costs are not in-cluded in the exhibition fee and will be billed as soon as possible after shipment.

Each Exhibitor is responsible for all local costs incurred in presenting the exhibition, including but not limited to its unpacking/repacking, crate storage, installation, publicity, programming, receptions, etc. Exhibitor is also responsible for any additional costs that may be specifically outlined in correspondence between The Sampler Museum and Exhibitor.

Main Negotiating Points

The fee itself: The exhibitor may want a discount, especially if the loan period is shortened or if only a part of the exhibition is shown for reasons beyond the control of either party. If the exhibitor wants a longer exhibition period, and it is possible within lender restrictions and the schedule, the fee should be increased.

Payment dates and number of installments: Fiscal years and fund-raising schedules differ, so it is important to be flexible about payment amounts and dates. For example, the exhibitor may want to make three payments, with the first made at signing, the second three to six months later, and the final at the beginning of the exhibition period, rather than the two payments often required by contracts. Having to make two large payments instead of three smaller ones, may force the exhibitor to delay the contract signing. The organizer should be sensitive to the exhibitor's budget schedule to ensure that the exhibition contract can be confirmed as early as possible.

Couriers: The borrowing institution will want information on the number of couriers that are expected from lending institutions, where they will be coming from, and whether they are needed for both installation and deinstallation.

Contract Standards

Payment of fees: Fees are usually divided into two or more installments. (See "Payment dates and number of installments.")

Couriers: The organizing museum's courier expense usually is included in the fee, and costs for lenders' couriers are not. If a decision to send a courier has not been made at the time the contract is negotiated, a clause covering such a situation can be included (e.g., "If the organizer decides to send a courier to oversee condition reporting and installation, the expense will be considered part of the exhibition fee.").

3. INSURANCE
Fine arts insurance
Indemnity
Immunity from seizure

Comment Insurance for the exhibition should be fine arts insurance, which covers the exhibition materials wall-to-wall, including when they are in transit. Fine arts insurance covers objects from the time they leave the owner's premises until the time they return there.

Usually the institution that produces the traveling exhibition insures it completely, either by relying on the organizing museum's fine arts (collections) policy or by purchasing a separate policy for the exhibition. A museum may prefer to obtain a separate policy to protect its primary policy from increased premiums or other adverse effects that may result from claims made during the exhibition's tour.

To share the assumption of risk, the organizer may insure the exhibition in transit to the first venue and require the exhibitor to insure, on condition checking, while the exhibition is on premises and during the next transit, repeating the transfer of insurance at each subsequent venue. Some lenders prefer to insure their own pieces while they are in the exhibition. If the exhibition is composed of very high value domestic loans or is borrowed primarily from foreign lenders, the organizing museum may decide to apply for the indemnity offered by the US government. (See chapter 3.)

Contract Language
The Sampler Museum, as part of the exhibition loan fee, shall continuously insure the exhibition materials on a wall-to-wall basis against all risks of physical loss or damage from any external cause except wear and tear, gradual deterioration, terrorism, and other exclusions standard to fine arts policies. Exhibitor shall report immediately to the Registrar, The Sampler Museum, any damage to the exhibition materials while in transit to or on the premises of Exhibitor, regardless of who is responsible. Contact the Registrar at 001-000-0000.

Exhibitor must preserve all parts, packing materials, and other evidence or result of damage and provide photographs and a written report documenting damage and action taken in response.

Comment Two further risks must be covered: negligence on the part of the exhibitor and a situation in which the organizing institution does not receive adequate payment to cover damage. The organizing institution generally waives subrogation for the exhibitor or names the exhibitor as "additionally insured" but may include language holding the exhibitor responsible for negligence or noncompliance.

Contract Language
The Sampler Museum shall waive subrogation against Exhibitor or name Exhibitor as "additionally insured." Exhibitor may be held responsible for damage to exhibition materials that results from its negligence or failure to comply with this agreement, including but not limited to its failure to comply with The Sampler Museum's registration notes and instructions regarding security, unpacking/repacking, handling, installation/deinstallation and shipment, as well as any and all loss of or damage to the exhibition materials occurring during the loan period that The Sampler Museum does not recover from an insurance carrier.

Comment If desired, this section can also discuss Immunity from Seizure, which is a request that the federal government protect art and artifacts on loan from foreign countries from seizure. Seizure is a remedy used sometimes when there are questions of ownership or when a claim for repatriation is made. It is prudent to request immunity from seizure for any imported material. To be valid, immunity must be granted prior to importation of the material.

Main Negotiating Points
Immunity from seizure: An application for foreign loans can be negotiated by the organizing institution, and if there is a foreign venue, the organizing museum may require immunity from seizure from the government of that venue.

Insurance costs: Exhibitors may negotiate if insurance is an added expense for them.

Terrorism insurance: This can be bought in some instances; the price of the insurance and thus the fee for the exhibition might rise in this case.

Notes and instructions: Exhibitor may ask that the registration notes and other instructions be available for review before the contract is signed. These notes can be an addendum to the contract or delivered separately. Ideally, they should be supplied before the contract is signed, but they *must* be provided before the exhibition materials are delivered. The exhibitor may wish to stipulate a date in the contract for delivery of these notes and instructions (e.g., three months before opening of the exhibition).

Contract Standards

Insurance: The organizing institution normally buys and maintains insurance. If not, other arrangements for ensuring continuous insurance of exhibition objects must be clearly described.

Waivers of subrogation: If a waiver of subrogation is requested, it should be carefully reviewed and discussed with the insurance provider before it is granted.

4. EXHIBITION DISPLAY/RESTRICTIONS

Comment This section of the contract lays out the organizer's expectations regarding the exhibitor's use of the exhibition. The organizer usually asks that the entire exhibition be shown unless there is a written agreement to the contrary. This requirement is especially important for thematic exhibitions. This section also usually states that the exhibitor agrees to abide by care and handling regulations set forth by the organizer.

Contracts with the Smithsonian Institution's Traveling Exhibition Service (SITES) have language regulating the use of the exhibition and the fees that can be charged, including the following paragraph:

The Exhibitor shall use the Exhibition only for educational purposes; no commercial or political uses may be made of the Exhibition. Neither the name of the Exhibition nor the name of [Organizing Museum] may be used in conjunction with any fund-raising or political event. With prior permission of [Organizing Museum], a special entrance fee may be charged to offset the costs of the Exhibition.

It may be important to put information about fees into the contract, whether they are allowed or discouraged. There is a trend, especially with blockbuster exhibitions, for the organizer to ask the exhibitor to return part of the gate receipts for the exhibition, sometimes as much as 60 percent. If a museum does not charge an entrance fee, the organizer may increase the participation fee to meet its income expectations.

Contract Language

Exhibitor shall exhibit all objects and exhibition materials as listed in Appendix A, unless express written permission to the contrary has been obtained in advance from The Sampler Museum. Exhibitor will not show the Exhibition at more than one location without prior written permission from The Sampler Museum. The Sampler Museum may withdraw or replace an object or objects in the exhibition at any time for any reason.

Furthermore, Exhibitor agrees to provide a secure and environmentally suitable storage area (as outlined in the care and handling regulations, Appendix B) for any exhibition materials withdrawn from the Exhibition for any reason and/or to pay any additional transportation or courier costs which may be incurred as a result of withdrawals of exhibition materials from the Exhibition.

The Sampler Museum shall provide Exhibitor with a detailed set of guidelines for the handling and display of exhibition objects and materials [amount of time] before the opening of the Exhibition. Exhibitor shall make such guidelines accessible to its installation and design staff, and to other applicable staff, and shall be responsible for ensuring strict adherence to such guidelines.

Main Negotiating Points

The exhibition of the entire group of objects is often a requirement set forth in an exhibition contract. If objects are withdrawn or added, negotiations should occur.

Care and handling: There may be a need to negotiate some of the care and handling requirements or the responsibilities for some items in the guidelines (e.g., microclimate boxes). Problems with space may arise. The exhibitor, for example, may not be able to store crates in a humidity-controlled environment and may ask for longer acclimation periods as an alternative.

Comment The organizer must establish care and handling guidelines, which should include information about light levels, environmental concerns (RH and temperature levels), which staff are allowed to handle materials, storage for exhibition crates, notes about condition and conservation procedures, installation guidelines for microclimates, vitrine materials, mount and installation hardware specifications, general security requirements, and any specific problems for mounting or handling known by the organizer. These guidelines can be included in the contract proper, as an addendum, or as a document that is drawn up later and sent to the exhibitor.

Withdrawal of exhibition material is often a vital point of negotiation, especially in a thematic exhibition. Exhibitors sometimes wish to add material to an exhibition as well; such material may be incorporated in the main exhibition or in a separate, smaller exhibition produced by the exhibitor. In the former case, especially if the exhibition is thematic, the exhibitor should work closely with the organizer's exhibition curator.

5. CREDIT LINES/SPONSORSHIPS

Comment   Credit lines are important to the exhibition's funders and, if applicable, to commercial sponsors. The organizing institution must ensure that these funders and sponsors are credited as the exhibition travels from site to site. The credit information should be stated explicitly and completely in the contract.

Contract Language

The following credit shall be included on invitations and official press releases and posted at the entrance to the exhibition.

Sample the Future was organized by The Sampler Museum, Any Town, Any State. The exhibition has received funding from the National Endowment for the Humanities and the New Foundation. Additional support has been received from foundations, corporations, and individuals.

Other promotional and related programmatic materials must carry the first sentence of the above credit.

Main Negotiating Points

Length of credit: The exhibitor may want a shorter credit line, especially for invitations.

Font size may be specified.

Commercial sponsors usually will want to be named first, and many will ask that their logos be used. This will alter the image of all materials and may be a point of negotiation with exhibitors.

Local sponsors: If the exhibitor seeks additional sponsorships locally, the organizer may want to negotiate about placement of local versus tour credit information.

6. SHIPPING
Fees
Exhibition materials
Couriers

Comment   Shipping costs generally are separated from the exhibition fee. Shipping methods should be clearly spelled out in the contract and an estimate for shipping given. The estimate should be "worst-case scenario," and the exhibition organizer should not charge more than that estimate. Shipping may be one-way (or "one leg," that is, the cost only to next venue) or prorated (divided among exhibiting institutions on the basis of their relative distances from the organizer's location), and methods of shipping will depend on the size, value, and fragility of the exhibition as well as the venues to which it is going. Given the vagaries of tour schedules and the disparate distances between venues, the organizer should be flexible about types of shipping charges. The following example calls for prorated shipping. (See also chapter 5.)

Contract Language

Exhibitor is responsible for the cost of shipping, which will be prorated among all exhibitors. The estimated cost of shipping is $7,500 and is payable upon receipt of the exhibition. Adjustments to shipping payments will be made at the end of the Exhibition's tour.

For foreign venues, and for Alaska and Hawaii, the Exhibitor must pay incoming/outgoing shipping costs from/to the selected port of exit and entry in the contiguous 48 states of the United States in addition to the prorated shipping costs. The foreign exhibitor also is required to pay all charges for customs clearance of the Exhibition leaving or reentering the United States.

The Sampler Museum or the previous Exhibitor shall pack the exhibition materials for shipment to the Exhibitor and arrange for their delivery to Exhibitor no later than the first day of the loan period by a carrier selected and scheduled in advance by The Sampler Museum. Exhibitor agrees to meet all transportation schedules required for the safety of objects and the timely shipment to other exhibitors. Exhibitor agrees that if it is unable to receive and ship the Exhibition in compliance with the necessary transportation schedule, it will absorb the cost of an acceptable interim storage facility and other expenses resulting from its inability to comply with such schedule.

Main Negotiating Points

Dates of transport: Exhibitor will ask for, and should be part of, negotiations concerning dates of transport. Both parties should be as flexible as possible regarding shipment dates.

Storage: Costs for interim storage may have to be clarified.

Date of arrival: The exhibitor usually wants as much time as possible before the opening date to unpack and install the exhibition.

Contract Standards

Shipping costs: Prorating costs for shipment is usual. Creative solutions will be required for exhibitions with gaps between venues or that travel to only one other venue. The exhibitor may be required to pay the one-way shipment to the next venue. Or, in some cases, round-trip shipping.

Carriers: The organizing institution makes all decisions regarding carriers and staff accompanying for shipments between venues and for staff accompanying the exhibition. Staff from the organizing museum work with exhibitors to set up workable dates for pickups and deliveries. Lenders, as noted previously, also may send couriers to the exhibiting venues.

7. PACKING/HANDLING/CARE/CONDITION REPORTING
Contract Language
Exhibitor shall ensure that all packing and unpacking instructions given by The Sampler Museum are followed explicitly by competent packers who are trained in museum object handling and that the exhibition materials are handled with special care at all times to protect against damage or deterioration. All unloading, unpacking, handling, repacking and reloading shall occur under the surveillance of the Exhibitor's registrar, or other designated courier, in consultation with the Exhibitor's conservators and security staff, or applicable staff. Exhibition objects may not be handled by volunteers or interns. Exhibition material shall be handled with at least the same care as Exhibitor uses in handling its own property of a similar nature.

In preparing exhibition materials for their outgoing shipment, Exhibitor shall ensure that they are packed in the same manner with the same or equivalent wrapping materials in which they were delivered to Exhibitor. Exhibition materials shall be prepared for outgoing shipment before the scheduled shipment date, which shall occur no later than the last day of the loan period. Exhibitor shall notify immediately, by telephone, text, or e-mail, the Registrar of The Sampler Museum about any loss or damage to the packing materials or packing crates that might impair in any way its ability to protect the exhibition materials. At its own expense and in consultation with the Registrar of The Sampler Museum, Exhibitor shall replace packing materials or crates lost or damaged while in its care with comparable materials.

Exhibitor must examine the exhibition materials after a 24-hour acclimation period and within seven days of their receipt and report on their condition. Each object will be accompanied by an illustrated condition report, which will be annotated as appropriate and signed by Exhibitor's conservator or registrar and by an authorized representative of the Organizer and/or lender representative present at unpacking, installation, deinstallation, and repacking on Exhibitor's premises. The Sampler Museum has deemed it necessary for a Sampler representative to be present for the unpacking, installation, deinstallation, and repacking of the Exhibition. Exhibitor will ensure that the condition reports travel with the objects to the next Exhi-

bition site; that the condition of the objects is checked regularly while in Exhibitor's possession; and that any significant change in an object's condition while in the possession of the Exhibitor is noted on the report and reported immediately to The Sampler Museum. The condition reports will be the only official record of changes in the objects' condition.

If any damage to the objects is discovered at any time during the loan period, written reports, accompanied by photographic documentation must be sent immediately to the Registrar of The Sampler Museum. Exhibitor agrees that it may not alter or repair any of the exhibition materials without first obtaining the express written permission of The Sampler Museum.

Main Negotiating Points
Staff: Discussions about unpacking or packing personnel will occur if the borrowing institution does not have a registrar. This may, in some instances, lead to a decision to send a registrar/installation specialist from the organizing institution. It may also lead to hiring a qualified contract registrar in the exhibitor's location.
Crates: A period of time before opening the crates may be negotiated if there is a delay in schedule, or if crates must move from off-site to on-site storage. This clause should have careful consideration because it is inadvisable for museum objects to stay in travel crates for long periods of time. Although crate materials should be of high quality, they are almost never inert, and eventual breakdown of the materials can lead to object deterioration.
Environmental requirements: It is not usual but it may occasionally be necessary for the organizer to negotiate environmental requirements with the lender. This necessity may arise with foreign loans, where environmental standards may differ substantially from US standards.

Contract Standards
Crates: Generally, crates are not opened until 24–48 hours after delivery to ensure that they acclimate to their new surroundings. Three to seven days is generally the maximum allowable delay before they are opened. Anything longer than that should be negotiated.
Handling standards are similar to those in a general loan agreement (i.e., handling should be done by trained personnel and not volunteers or interns) and the organizer must be notified if there are any problems.
Repacking should be in the same crates, using the same or equivalent materials as the original packing.

Organizer must provide good information about packing and crate lists so that this can be done properly. If packing notes are not provided, the exhibitor should create detailed documentation while unpacking takes place to return the exhibition packed exactly as it was received.

8. FACILITIES
Security
Environment

Comment The organizing institution should use this section for outlining the security and environment controls that are expected of the borrowing institution. Information about general security and environment should be expanded with special considerations for high-value or highly sensitive artifacts. All borrowing institutions should be asked to provide a *General Facility Report*, available from the American Alliance of Museums (AAM), to the organizing institution for review. This section of the contract also may refer to laws on discrimination and disabilities.

SITES has developed careful guidelines for low- to high-value exhibitions and uses the following definitions:

Limited Security:

1. defined interior exhibition space other than a passageway
2. continuous surveillance of the exhibition during public hours
3. locked and secured conditions at all other times

Moderate Security:

1. a limited-access gallery space
2. continuous surveillance by trained staff or professional guards during public hours
3. locked and secured conditions at all other times
4. secured, locked exhibition cases
5. handling by trained museum personnel
6. constant temperature of 68°–72° F
7. lighting levels adjustable to eight to ten foot-candles

High Security:

1. a limited-access gallery space
2. continuous surveillance by trained museum guards in each room or area of the exhibition during public hours

3. guards and/or electronic alarm system at all other times
4. installation designed to protect each exhibition component from physical contact
5. locked and secured exhibition cases
6. handling by trained professional museum personnel
7. constant temperature of 68°–72° F
8. constant relative humidity of 45–50 percent
9. lighting levels adjustable to five to eight foot-candles

Contract Language

Exhibitor shall, at its own expense, provide adequate security and environmental conditions for the exhibition materials and shall comply with any and all special instructions put forth by The Sampler Museum for the care of the exhibition objects and materials. Exhibitor shall provide The Sampler Museum with a copy of its General Facility Report (GFR), available from the American Alliance of Museums. The Sampler Museum will evaluate the GFR as part of the contract review process.

All objects must be displayed according to guidelines provided by the organizer. The Exhibitor shall assign security guard(s) to the exhibition space during open hours, as required in the guidelines. As a security minimum during closed hours, Exhibitor must have electronic surveillance systems that report to a central station that is manned 24 hours a day. Permission to use plants in the galleries must be obtained from the Registrar of The Sampler Museum; food and drink must NOT be allowed in the exhibition galleries, storage areas, or anywhere the exhibition objects and materials are kept.

The Exhibitor shall maintain 50% ± 5% relative humidity and 68°–72° F. Light levels shall be maintained according to the guidelines provided.

The public shall be admitted to the exhibition without discrimination or segregation, and regardless of race, color, creed, sex, age, or national origin. In addition, the Exhibitor represents that there is full access to the exhibition for the physically disabled, as stipulated in Section 504 of Federal Public Law 93-112, as amended. Exhibitor shall be in compliance with the Americans with Disabilities Act (Public Law 101-336, enacted July 26, 1990).

Comments Use this section to define security according to the low, medium, or high value of the exhibition. The sample language covers an exhibition of medium value. Contracts for high-value exhibitions will require more security, perhaps specific sound and motion detectors, security personnel in each exhibition area, continuous visual surveillance, or special storage arrangements. Low-value exhibitions may allow volunteer or singly manned galleries, no central systems, perhaps even a wider environmental range.

It is vital that the organizing institution provide clear guidelines and either include them in or append them to the contract.

Main Negotiating Points

Environmental guidelines may be negotiated. Some lenders may require a higher standard of relative humidity or may require it only for fragile artifacts; the Exhibitor may not be able to meet those standards.

Alarms: Number and types of alarms should be discussed.

Security: Number and positions of security personnel should be discussed.

Contract Standards

American environmental standards remain 50% ± 5% relative humidity and 68°–72° F. European museums often request higher relative humidity.

9. PUBLICITY
Catalogs
Promotion
Photography

Contract Language

The Sampler Museum will supply Exhibitor with a press release and a selection of photographic images that may be used in preparing publicity and related materials for the Exhibition. Exhibitor agrees to clear its own press releases and publicity materials, including those used on social media, with the Public Relations department of The Sampler Museum before use.

Exhibitor shall forward promptly to The Sampler Museum's contact person all publicity releases, reviews, and other similar matter relating to the exhibition. At the end of the loan period, Exhibitor will forward attendance figures and visitor feedback to The Sampler Museum.

The Sampler Museum reserves the right to copy, photograph, or reproduce exhibition objects and materials. Exhibitor shall not permit any of the exhibition objects and materials to be copied, photographed, or reproduced without prior written consent from The Sampler Museum. In the event of the public exhibition of the objects, Exhibitor shall contain in its photography guidelines the following statement: "Unless prohibited by any relevant copyright holders, visitors are permitted to take informal photographs using handheld cameras without flash. Tripods and monopod extension poles ("selfie sticks") are prohibited. Visitors may not take professional photographs in the Exhibition." Exhibitor agrees to take all such action as may be reasonably necessary to enforce such policy.

Notwithstanding the foregoing statement, Exhibitor may photograph exhibition objects and materials for curatorial and registrarial purposes, provided that such photographs are made without removal of frames or mounts and are not released to the public without The Sampler Museum's prior written consent and provided that The Sampler Museum is supplied with a DVD of such images.

The Sampler Museum will provide Exhibitor with 15 copies of the catalog *Sample the Future*. Additional copies of the catalog can be purchased at cost from The Sampler Museum Shop.

Main Negotiating Points

Catalogs: The number of catalogs and their delivery dates may be a point of discussion.

Contract Standards

Catalogs: It is usual for a number of catalogs (five to ten) to be included in the exhibition fee. Borrowing institutions often receive a discount when purchasing additional catalogs; the complete price and ordering information should be detailed in the contract.

Attendance figures and visitor feedback usually are forwarded at the end of the exhibition.

Photography: It is usual practice to allow no photography of borrowed exhibitions or exhibition objects. However, because of the nearly universal availability of cell phones, and because of the publicity value of social-media posts from exhibitions, many museums no longer stringently forbid photography. Copyright concerns, the integrity of the exhibition, and safety of objects are still at issue.

SECTIONS 10–20 These sections are fairly standard to traveling exhibition contracts. Section 10, "Damages, Breach of Agreement," is the section most open to interpretation and negotiation. The other sections, except for the section on governing law, are generally not negotiable. Governing law, however, is sometimes a matter of contention between legal counsel of the organizing and borrowing parties. Some museums absolutely will not sign a contract with the governing law outside of their own state. One way around this objection is to drop the clause altogether and worry about it only if there is a problem with a contract. However, the clause should not be changed or left out in a contract with a foreign venue.

10. DAMAGES, BREACH OF AGREEMENT

Comment   This section attempts to determine fair remedies if one or the other of the parties cannot complete its responsibilities as part of the contract. It also includes payments and financial remedies that should be put in place if there are problems with contract. This section is important and should be carefully written, reviewed, and negotiated because cancellation by one of the Exhibitors is the most often encountered problem with a traveling exhibition contract.

This section also includes the withdrawal of one or more objects from the exhibition and the duties of both parties should a withdrawal become necessary.

Contract Language

Exhibitor must notify The Sampler Museum in writing to cancel the signed Agreement. The parties understand that it will be difficult, if not impossible, to calculate or estimate the serious and substantial damage to The Sampler Museum which would be caused by breach of this Agreement by Exhibitor. Therefore, the parties agree that in the event Exhibitor cancels this Agreement prior to the beginning of the loan period, for any reason whatsoever (other than the inability of The Sampler Museum to perform hereunder), Exhibitor shall pay to The Sampler Museum, as liquidated damages and not as a penalty, the total loan fee, which balance shall be due and payable immediately upon such cancellation. However, in the event that Exhibitor or The Sampler Museum arranges for an alternate venue for the Exhibition acceptable to The Sampler Museum during the loan period, the fees received from that venue, less the cost of procuring such alternate venue, shall be applied to reduce the amount payable to The Sampler Museum under this paragraph. The Sampler Museum, however, shall have no obligation to procure such alternate sponsor, and the Exhibitor is entitled to no reduction of the loan fee for The Sampler Museum's failure to procure such alternate venue.

In the event Exhibitor fails to pay any amount when due under this Agreement, including but not limited to costs payable under sections 1 and 2 above, such failure continuing for a period of 10 business days, the amount at the rate of 15% per annum from the date the unpaid amount originally was due will accrue until the late payment is received by The Sampler Museum. Nothing in this Agreement shall be construed as an expressed or implied agreement by The Sampler Museum to forbear in the collection of any delinquent payment. Furthermore, this Agreement shall not be construed as in any way giving Exhibitor the right, expressed or implied, to fail to make timely payments hereunder, whether upon payment of such interest rate or otherwise. Should Exhibitor not remit the first payment before the scheduled shipment date, The Sampler Museum reserves the right to cancel the contract at its own discretion.

The parties further understand that, while The Sampler Museum shall endeavor to make all reasonable effort to assure delivery of the Exhibition to Exhibitor prior to the scheduled opening as stated above:

a) In the event that The Sampler Museum is unable to perform hereunder, The Sampler Museum shall promptly refund to Exhibitor the fee already paid by Exhibitor in full and complete satisfaction of its obligation to Exhibitor. Upon prior written notice, The Sampler Museum may terminate this Agreement prior to the beginning of the loan period for events beyond its control. Exhibitor shall release, indemnify, and hold The Sampler Museum harmless from and against any and all loss arising from Exhibitor's inability to display the Exhibition because of loss or damage to the exhibition objects and materials while in transit; and

b) in the event The Sampler Museum for any reason withdraws any object from the Exhibition while it is in circulation, Exhibitor shall promptly comply with all packing and shipping instructions given by The Sampler Museum in the course of such withdrawal. The Sampler Museum shall concurrently reimburse Exhibitor for its costs and the expenses of packing and shipping incurred by such withdrawal.

No waiver by either party of any failure by the other party to keep or perform any covenant or condition of this Agreement shall be deemed to be a waiver of any preceding or succeeding breach of the same or any other covenant or condition of this Agreement.

In the case of any uncertainty regarding the language contained within this agreement, the language shall be construed in accordance with its fair meaning and not interpreted against the party who caused the uncertainty to exist.

11. NOTICES

Comment   It is prudent to list all primary contact information in this section of the contract, for instance:

If to The Sampler Museum:
Name and title
Address
Phone

Mobile
E-mail

If to the Exhibitor:
Name and title
Address
Phone
Mobile
E-mail

Contract Language

Except as otherwise specifically required herein, all notices and other communication provided for or permitted hereunder shall be made by hand-delivery; prepaid, first-class mail; fax; or e-mail. All notices are considered delivered when delivered by hand, four days after deposit of first-class mail, and when receipt is acknowledged for fax and e-mail. In the case of extreme emergencies, immediate verbal consent should be sought by Exhibitor and followed as soon as possible in writing.

12. SUCCESSORS AND ASSIGNS
Contract Language

The Agreement shall inure to the benefit of and be binding upon the successors of each of the parties. This Agreement may not be assigned by either party without the prior written consent of the other.

13. WAIVERS, REMEDIES
Contract Language

No delay on the part of any party hereto in exercising any right, power, or privilege hereunder shall operate as a waiver thereof, nor shall any waiver on the part of any party hereto of any right, power, or privilege hereunder operate as a waiver of any right, power, or privilege hereunder.

14. ENTIRE AGREEMENT
Contract Language

This Agreement, together with all written special instructions accompanying the Exhibition, is intended by the parties as a final expression of their agreement and is a complete and exclusive statement of the agreement and understanding of the parties. This Agreement supersedes all prior agreements and understandings between the parties with respect to the subject matter contained herein.

15. ATTORNEYS' FEES
Contract Language

In any action or proceeding brought to enforce any provision of this Agreement, or where any provision

hereof is validly asserted as a defense, the successful party shall be entitled to recover reasonable attorneys' fees in addition to any other available remedy.

16. SEVERABILITY
Contract Language

In the event that any one or more of the provisions contained herein, or the application thereof in any circumstances, is held invalid, illegal, or unenforceable in any respect for any reason, the validity, legality, and enforceability of any such provision in every other respect and of the remaining provisions hereof shall not in any way be impaired or affected, it being intended that all of the rights and privileges contained herein shall be enforceable to the fullest extent permitted by law.

17. GOVERNING LAW
Contract Language

This Agreement shall be governed by and construed in accordance with laws of the State of Any State.

18. DISPUTE RESOLUTION
Contract Language

Any dispute or difference arising out of or in connection with this contract shall be determined by the appointment of a single arbitrator to be agreed between the parties, or failing agreement within fourteen days, after either party has given to the other a written request to concur in the appointment of an arbitrator, by an arbitrator to be appointed by American Arbitration Association [*or other appropriately applicable arbitration body*].

19. SIGNATURES

Comment A place must be provided for signatures and titles of the officers who have the authority to sign the contract for both the organizing museum and the borrowing venue. Some contracts request that signatures be notarized; in rare instances, the borrowing institution may be required to provide documentation of the authority of the signing officer.

20. APPENDIXES/ATTACHMENTS/SCHEDULES

Comment Two important appendixes must be added to the contract: a precise and complete list of all of the objects in the exhibition and a listing of the venues with confirmed bookings. Care and handling guidelines can be included within the contract, under packing/handling/care/condition reporting, or there can be a brief statement in that section (as noted in section 7) and the complete handling and environmental requirements included in an appendix.

4-2 NEGOTIATING CONTRACTS

Negotiating Personnel

The museum's size and organization dictates the negotiating process for a contract for a traveling exhibition. Museums use different models to coordinate exhibitions and administer projects; it is vital that one person be responsible for all aspects of an exhibition's coordination, including negotiation of the contract. The organizing institution should designate a person to negotiate with exhibitors, and that person must keep in mind that different exhibitors review contracts in different ways. The negotiator should also be in charge of internal coordination and have thorough knowledge of the loan agreements the institution has made with lenders.

Model 1: Many museums have a designated coordinator of exhibitions. That person may be an exhibitions manager, a deputy director, or a senior curator or registrar. The title and place in the organizational chart depend on the individual museum. The coordinator is responsible for managing all in-house aspects of an exhibition.

Model 2: Some museums have designated project directors who are responsible for all aspects of an exhibition assigned to them; they are the head negotiators for contracts for their projects and they oversee the completion and control the quality of the project.

Model 3: A lone administrator, with some assistance from other staff, determines the contract, schedule, and implementation of the exhibition.

If a museum has a large enough budget to afford a coordinator of exhibitions, Model 1 is preferred. A person who is a capable administrator, someone who knows the parameters of the exhibition and has experience in all aspects of the exhibition process, is without doubt the most effective person to take charge of this complex process. In addition, several staff members must be aware of the contents and terms of the contract and have a voice in the final negotiations. These staff members include the director, principal curator, registrar, director of external affairs, exhibition designer, conservator, editor (for the label content, text panels, publications), museum store manager (for supplies of catalogs and other merchandise), public relations officer, and business manager.

Disclosures

The organizer must know as much as possible about the physical plant of the exhibitor before contracting the exhibition. The contract should be contingent on the organizer's review and acceptance of the *General Facilities Report*, available from the AAM, as completed by the exhibitor. It is also a good idea to ask for a copy of the emergency response plan in place at the borrowing institution.

Negotiation Process

A representative from the borrowing institution writes a letter of intent or calls the organizing institution to declare interest in booking the exhibition.

The organizing institution sends the potential exhibitor the contract, which the exhibitor circulates among its various departments.

The registrar's office should weigh in on collection care, insurance, shipping, storage, and the environment. That office also will prepare a *General Facilities Report* to send to the organizer.

The exhibition designer should review clauses on design, integrity of the exhibition layout, case and mount provision, and lighting.

The marketing staff should review credits, photography, rights and reproduction clauses, and material pertaining to press releases and local support.

Educators should be aware of clauses pertaining to partnering with the organizing institution in educational programs and of educational materials available to exhibition borrowers.

Administrators should review the fees and schedules and work with the coordinator of exhibitions to determine the best dates for the exhibition. The fiscal year of the borrowing institution must be taken into consideration when negotiating payment schedules for exhibition and shipping fees.

The exhibitor's contact person comes back to the organizer with questions and concerns. A final contract is drawn up after agreement is reached on all points, and the exhibitor again circulates the contract for final review. When there is consensus, the contract is updated by the organizing institution and sent in duplicate to the exhibitor; the officer in charge at the borrowing institution signs and returns the contract to the organizing institution, customarily with payment of half of the exhibition fee.

CHAPTER 5

Preparing the Exhibition for the Tour

5-1 CRATES

Checklist for Crates

1. Determine which objects in the exhibition should be crated for travel.
2. Prepare a request for proposal (RFP) for the crate maker.
3. Choose a crate maker.
4. Arrange for delivery of crates made off-site.
5. Number each crate that will travel, both borrowed and newly made.
6. Measure each crate.
7. Make labels for each crate.
8. Make list of the objects in each crate.
9. Write packing instructions for each crate; use illustrations as needed.
10. Produce a master crate list with crate number, size, and objects contained.

1. DETERMINE WHICH OBJECTS IN THE EXHIBITION SHOULD BE CRATED FOR TRAVEL During the planning and consolidation phase of the exhibition, the registrar arranges to have crates made for objects from the organizer's permanent collection and determines whether crates for borrowed objects can travel or whether traveling crates must be built. For example, an object may have arrived from a lender soft-packed in acid-free tissue and bubble wrap. For its safe travel to several venues, however, it must be carefully cavity-packed and supported by foam in a crate or box sturdy enough to withstand handling and multiple openings and closings.

The crates should be sturdy and built to travel specifications. Travel crates should have bolt plates and not screws and definitely not nails; bolt plates should be used on internal braces as well as for closure. Crates should be fully waterproof, have good gaskets, and should be fitted with the proper amount of ester foam, placed to absorb the shock of possible hits or falls. It is important to lacquer or use water-based polyurethane on the exterior and interior of a traveling crate so that it does not warp easily as it moves through various climates. Coating only one side may increase the risk of the crate's warping. Coating the inside also slows down the off-gassing of the wood. Less damage to objects results, too, if interior braces and closures are not adjustable; plastic straps, rather than Tyvek ties, will exert the same amount of pressure on an object at each use.

Use basic references and current sources of information listed in the bibliography and, most important, the crate-maker's knowledge and experience to ensure that crates meet current standard. Standards and materials have changed over time and will continue to evolve as advancements in the field are made. Through its website and publications, the Preparation, Art Handling, Collections Care Information Network (PACCIN) is one of the best sources of information on this subject.

If a series of small paintings is included in the exhibition, it might be safer and more economical to build a single crate that can hold four or five paintings. Such cases can be made for prints, textiles, and small objects, as well. However, consider that wider and larger crates may not fit in small elevators and doorways and may be much heavier than single-object crates, adding unwanted risk. Crates with multiple objects are practical if the objects within them will not rotate in and out of the exhibition. In addition, the lender always has the right to decide how his or her object should travel, and that negotiation should take place before shipment to the first venue occurs.

For an object traveling a short distance, it might be possible to use a soft-pack for the initial delivery and then crate the piece with similar items for the trips to subsequent venues. If this is done, remember that the original packing materials must be marked and carefully stored so that they can be used for dispersal (i.e., the last shipment from the organizing institution to the lenders) at the end of the tour. Include a note about the original packing in the database. In some instances, it will be best to place all of the works in matching crates. This approach makes it possible to combine similarly sized objects into a single crate to reduce the total number of crates. Crates of the same color can aid the visual identification of the shipment in a poorly lighted airfreight warehouse and can make it easier to keep the shipment together. It also presents a single opening and closing method, for which a single set of tools can be provided, a useful feature when shipping to foreign venues.

2. PREPARE AN RFP FOR THE CRATE MAKER An RFP establishes specifications and standards to guide a contractor in making cost estimates. The RFP for the crate maker should include the complete exhibition list with sizes of all objects noted. Sizes for framed or rolled pieces or those with special mounts should also be included. Decide as early as possible if panels, labels, and cases or furniture traveling with the exhibition can be soft-packed, or if they, too, should be crated. However, if the exhibition will travel overseas, everything must be crated. Give the crate maker the exact specifications for the crates and discuss them with the crate maker before reaching a final agreement. The RFP should specify if the crates should be painted a specific color or require special stenciling or labels.

The RFP should also contain information about how and where the exhibition will be shipped. Factors such as the size of cargo bay doors on the specific aircraft to be used may require modification of usual crating specifications. A large piece may have to be crated with less than the optimal amount of cushioning material to fit into a certain conveyance. Crates that will travel to Europe must have wood that meets European Union (EU) requirements; this wood has been specifically heat treated and stamped with proper markings or made with man-made wood products such as plywood, which kills pests in the manufacturing process so that the crates only need to be stenciled that they are 100 percent plywood.

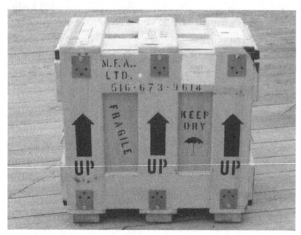

A typical traveling exhibition crate.

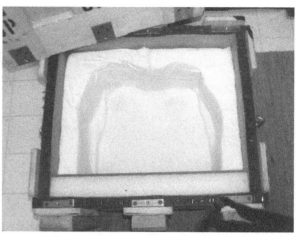

Inside of crate showing cavity pack.

The crater usually will visit the museum to see the objects—most easily done if the organizing museum is also the initial venue—and then provide a list of crates, sizes, and attendant costs. Often, the museum will have an ongoing relationship with a specific crater and will work out a crating contract with that firm. If possible, however, it is always prudent to seek two or three estimates.

If the organizing registrar and a lender agree that a piece (or pieces) should be crated separately, it is wise to review travel crate specifications with that lender, who then can arrange for crates made to those specifications. In that way, it is unlikely that the crates will have to be remade or replaced during the exhibition's run.

Other factors that the crater must consider include the type of glazing of framed objects, whether the objects have friable material, and whether works need to be packed vertically or horizontally, face up or face down. The crater also needs to be aware of any objects with extensive restorations that could influence where pads can contact the object. Finally, the crater needs to know from the start if some of the objects will not travel to all venues.

3. CHOOSE A CRATE MAKER The choice will be made largely on quoted price. However, such factors as construction standards, delivery and packing options, reliability, and past positive association with the crate maker may override small differences in price.

4. ARRANGE FOR DELIVERY OF CRATES MADE OFF-SITE Once a crate maker is chosen, the schedule for completion of the crates and their delivery should be set up. It is important that the crates arrive at least 24 hours (preferably more) in the museum before scheduled packing so that they can acclimate. New crates should remain with lids open during acclimatization, if possible, to enable solvents and gasses to dissipate. Whether the timing is critical in other respects depends on how much space is available for crate storage and breakdown. It is a good idea to ask the crater for extra closure plates and bolts to be packed with condition reports and conservation supplies for large traveling exhibitions.

5. NUMBER EACH CRATE THAT WILL TRAVEL, BOTH BORROWED AND NEWLY MADE A simple numbering system should be used on the crates; sequential numbers might be the best system. If crates from different exhibitions are stored together, or if crates will be saved for future use, it will help to have a prefix that immediately identifies the exhibition for which the crate was made (e.g., SF for *Sample the Future*).

6. MEASURE EACH CRATE Museums traditionally state object measurements using the format: *height × width/ length × depth*. Remember, though, that most shipping companies use a different sequence to state crate measurements: *width/length × depth × height*. Fine arts shippers will be aware of museum standards, but to ensure that there is no confusion, include both the measurement and the dimension measured (e.g., 25 in. wide × 12 in. deep × 57 in. high). Keeping these details clear can be important in positioning a sensitive work correctly on a truck or airplane to minimize the effects of movement and vibration.

7. MAKE LABELS FOR EACH CRATE Labels should be large, clear, and attached securely to the crate. Protect them by encasing them in clear plastic mailing pouches or covering them with clear packing tape. It is a good idea to attach two labels to each crate. Each label should include complete information about both the shipping institution (the organizing museum or the previous venue) and the receiving institution, including contact names and telephone numbers at both institutions.

Each exhibitor should label the crates for travel to the next venue. If the organizer prefers to remain the shipper of record, that should be communicated to the venue sending the crates to the next site.

Crates should be marked to indicate proper orientation in shipment and to denote fragility. For identification and shipping company reference, the crate number and measurements should be written or stenciled onto the crates. Indicating the contents of the crate on a label on the outside aids the packing and unpacking process, but convenience should be weighed against any security risk that might be created by making the contents known. If the contents of a crate are extremely fragile, consider attaching tilt and tells, as well as shock indicators. Consider using simplified markings, such as "extremely fragile—terracotta"

without other details, to alert fine art movers without revealing specific information.

8. MAKE A LIST OF THE OBJECTS IN EACH CRATE Record a crate list as the exhibition is packed at the close of the first venue. A rough packing list may be drawn up before packing begins, but minor adjustments usually will be necessary. If objects are cavity packed, or must go in a particular slot to ride best, mark the number of the objects on the ester foam or on the area below the slot. Make certain that all mounts, panels, photographs, and labels are listed next to the objects on the crate list.

9. WRITE PACKING INSTRUCTIONS FOR EACH CRATE; USE ILLUSTRATIONS AS NEEDED It is important to provide packing instructions so that the interior of the crate remains the same each time it is packed for travel. Digital photographic packing instructions are worth the effort and can show things like Oz clips or removable braces. Detailed photographic instructions are especially crucial for sculptures with braces, small objects in cavity packs, and objects with many parts that have several layers of ester foam between them.

The corners of the crate will be marked by the crate maker so that the lid is put on exactly the same way, time after time. In regard to sculpture crates that come apart, it is good practice to either letter or number the corners. These indicators should be placed at all intersections: crate pallet, crate walls, and crate lid to ensure that the crate is reassembled correctly.

Photographs that accompany the packing instructions make it easier for everyone and help to minimize possible damage to the objects in the crate. The simpler the packing, the less chance there is that damage to objects will occur. A master list of packing notes is essential, but it is helpful also to attach photos and packing notes to the individual crates so that they are easily found and used. Close-up photo details can be useful to show precise placement; focus on unique areas, such as firing flaws, visible accession numbers, or glazing, to show proper alignment and reduce handling and guesswork during repacking.

10. PRODUCE A MASTER CRATE LIST WITH CRATE NUMBER, SIZE, AND OBJECTS CONTAINED Use the numbering sequence to list the crates, and include the size of each and the object(s) it contains. If it is possible to obtain a weight for the crates, include that, as well. Weights are most critical for shipments by air or international shipments. Concerns, such as special handling requirements, volume and door size of shipping vehicles, or the capacity of the loading dock at any venue,

The Mint Museum
Office of the Registrar
2730 Randolph Road, Charlotte, NC 28207
Tel: 704.337.2000 | Fax: 704.337.2101

CONDITION REPORT

Purpose: Loan to exhibit *Michael Sherrill Retrospective*

Lender: Mint Museum

PACKING NOTES

Crated: Yes / No   Crate number: _____   Size (in.): H: _____   W: _____   D: _____

Notes:
    After removing foam blocks, whole tray pulls out. Easier to install seating center post first.

PACKING IMAGES

Hanging hardware

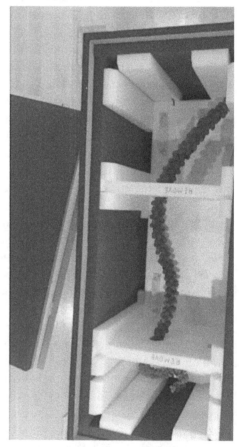

Page 1 of a Mint Museum electronic condition report showing packing notes.

should be discussed with the shipping company well in advance of the shipment date.

List the objects in each crate clearly, with exhibition number *and* all accession or temporary numbers that the object has been assigned.

The crate list (without object notes) should be included with the packet that goes to the shipping company, and it should be sent (with object notes) ahead of delivery to each exhibitor. Update the list if changes are made during the run of the exhibition, for example, if objects are rotated in and out.

5-2 SHIPPING

Checklist for Shipping the Exhibition between Venues
1. Draw up an RFP for shipping estimates.
2. Choose a shipping company.
3. Set up shipment to first venue.
4. Set up shipment from the first to the second venue, and so forth.
5. Decide whether to disperse from final venue or ship to organizing museum for dispersal.
6. Disperse exhibition.

Truck Shipments
Most traveling exhibitions within the United States are shipped by truck. Fine arts shipping companies use trucks that meet the prerequisites for exhibition travel: air ride, climate controlled, alarm equipped, and dual drivers. There are essentially three different types of truck service:

1. Shuttles
   Shuttles are regularly scheduled truck runs between cities, around regions, or from coast to coast. Small exhibitions of relatively low value may be shipped in this manner.

2. Last On, First Off
   With this service, the shipment goes onto the truck last and comes off first. This can be ordered (if conditions are perfect) with a shuttle, or with another run the company may be making. A direct shipment is necessary to make this possible (i.e., no other stops should be scheduled between the pickup from one venue and the delivery of the exhibition to the next).

3. Exclusive Use
   Exclusive use guarantees that the exhibition is the only cargo carried on the truck; no other jobs are consigned to the vehicle or drivers during the shipment period. It is the most expensive of the three types of truck shipments, but it is the one most often used to ship an entire exhibition. Fine arts shipping companies usually will allow a courier to ride with an exclusive-use shipment. If the exhibition is of high value, or if there is a large number of crates, this type of shipment is the best value.

The organizing museum should base the type of truck shipment it chooses on the size and value of the exhibition. Insurance transit maximums also should be taken into account. If the exhibition is worth $2 million and transit coverage on the policy covering the exhibition is $1 million, either obtain additional exhibition insurance coverage or divide the exhibition into two equal halves and ship it in two trucks. An extremely high-value or comprehensive exhibition, the total loss of which would obliterate an artist's life work or decimate a single collection, probably should be split into two units for all shipments, especially those by air.

Air Shipments
INTERNATIONAL SHIPPING Shipping within the contiguous forty-eight states generally is done by truck. When shipping to Alaska and Hawaii or overseas, air freight is the least problematic method. Transport by ship is used only when works are too large to fly, or when very large shipments of low-value material travel between coastal towns, for example, from Seattle to Anchorage.

For international shipments it is customary and wise to use a customs broker and freight forwarder who understands the requirements of customs clearance, has security credentials that allow him or her to be planeside to supervise loading, and has contacts in foreign cities who can provide the same services at the destination. Customs documents are difficult, the language and laws are opaque, and protection of the works is best left to those with good access to airports and an everyday understanding of the procedures and problems involved. Customs agents must be supplied with exact information about the works or objects that are scheduled to travel, including value, materials, and date of manufacture. Certain materials, such as ivory, must have special clearance to cross borders without problem; other objects simply cannot travel. The customs broker will have information about such situations and will also be aware of plane sizes, direct routes, and agents and carriers in the countries of destination who can receive the work and forward it to the exhibiting museum.

The originating museum will be asked to prepare a pro forma invoice for the shipment that includes information about the works and their origination, destination, and return. The invoice must be provided for the outgoing shipment so that it will be certified for the return shipment to the United States.

If a courier is traveling with the shipment, he or she should be well versed in courier practice. The courier should stay with the crates as much as possible, note pallet numbers, carry all relevant documentation, and keep high-nutrition protein bars and bottled water close by.

TSA CERTIFIED CARGO SCREENING PROGRAM On August 3, 2007, President George W. Bush signed into law the Implementing the 9/11 Commission Recommendations Act of 2007. This legislation required the Secretary of Homeland Security to establish within three years a system for screening 100 percent of cargo transported on passenger aircraft at a level of security commensurate with that of passenger checked baggage. The impact of the 100 percent screening requirement is that all cargo must be screened at the piece level approved methods by Transportation Safety Administration (TSA) prior to being loaded onto a passenger aircraft.

To help airlines reach this goal, the Certified Cargo Screening Standard Security Program (CCSSSP) allows manufacturers, warehouses, distribution centers, third-party logistics providers, indirect air carriers, airport cargo handlers, and independent cargo screening facilities, including museums and fine arts transport companies, to organize and conduct this screening of cargo before delivery to the airlines. Mu-

seums are eligible and encouraged, if they do significant passenger flight shipping, to become part of the program. Application, approval, inspection, and training are necessary for certification, but going through the process can allow a museum to control the safe handling and care of shipped objects.

Museums should consult their shipping agents to determine the best procedures to avoid opening crates at the airport, which include joining the CCSSSP or having a fine arts company perform the screening in their certified facility.

For further information, visit the TSA website at https://www.tsa.gov/for-industry/cargo-programs, or for questions about joining the CCSSSP, contact TSA-ContactCenter@tsa.dhs.gov.

Charging the Exhibitor for Shipments
As noted in chapter 4, the exhibitor is usually financially responsible for both the exhibition fees and the shipping costs. The organizing museum must decide whether to charge one-way shipping, a set rate, or prorated shipping costs to the borrowing institution. Be creative when making decisions about travel. Prorating (i.e., evenly dividing total costs among all the exhibitors) is common, although the organizer must decide whether to include consolidation shipment to the organizing institution and the dispersal at the end.

Charging for one-way shipment is another approach, with the exhibitor paying for the outgoing shipment to the next venue only. If there are gaps in the exhibition schedule, however, and the exhibition has to return to the organizer for storage, the exhibitor may be charged for a round-trip shipment.

RFPs
The organizer should make separate RFPs to obtain cost estimates for crating, consolidation, tour shipment, customs/forwarding, and dispersal. Although there are some firms that handle all aspects of crating and shipping, they are not found in all areas of the United States. Even if the organizer hires a single firm to perform all of these services, it is likely that some consolidation and dispersal will be done using varied shipment methods (e.g., air freight, museum truck/staff, lender delivery or pickup). To ensure lowest costs, it is wise to compare bids for services from more than one vendor in each area.

As soon as the itinerary is established, send an RFP to at least three shipping service providers. It should be done as early as possible and should include the following information:

Example Pro Forma Invoice

Shipping Institution:	Name and address
Consignee:	Name and address
Inventory:	
Artist (Maker)	
Title (Object Name), Date	
Media	
Dimensions	
Value	
Purpose:	For exhibition? For exhibition and return? For sale? For examination?
Declaration and Signature:	

THE SAMPLER MUSEUM

[letterhead]
Museum Service Representative
Museum Services Company
123 Museum Services Blvd.
Service Town, Any State 12345

Dear Museum Services Representative,

We are in the process of putting together a budget for our upcoming *Sample the Future* exhibition which opens in September 2020. We request estimates for shipping between venues and dispersal of the exhibition.

Please note:

- All vehicles must be climate controlled (70° F, ± 5°), dual driver (nonsmokers), air-ride (tractor and trailer suspension system), lift gate.
- All segments of the shipment must be exclusive use.
- The trucks must accommodate a courier on board, unless otherwise stated.
- The museum will be responsible for insuring this exhibition.

Itinerary:

September 26, 2020–January 2, 2021	The Sampler Museum
February 3, 2021–May 23, 2021	The Bangor Museum
June 25, 2021–October 1, 2021	Sarasota History and Cultural Center
November 3, 2021–February 6, 2021	Oslo Technical Museum

Note: Overseas Freight Forwarding Services will handle the international portion of the tour. The shipment from Sarasota, Florida, will be delivered to Far South International Airport on or about October 7, 2021. The shipment will return to Any Town International Airport on or about February 20, 2021, for shipment to The Sampler Museum. All dates are subject to confirmation.

Dispersal Information:
The crate designated for Italy (Crate # 16) will not travel from Oslo to The Sampler Museum. It will be shipped directly to Italy by Oslo Transport. Please pick up all other loans from the Sampler Museum and return them to the original lenders, unless otherwise specified. Attached is a complete list of lenders, with specific information about objects and how they are crated.

Request Summary:

1. Tour cost as outlined in itinerary.
2. Dispersal costs begin from The Sampler Museum, and all loans return to the original lenders, unless otherwise specified.
3. Grand total regarding cost of services.

Reminder:
Exclusive-use transportation is required unless otherwise specified. We ask that the van be climate controlled (maintaining a temperature of 70° F) and air-ride equipped; its lift gate must have the capacity to handle our shipment requirements. In addition, we require dual driver (nonsmokers) service.

Please let me know if you have questions regarding this request for proposal. I look forward to your response, which we would like to receive no later than September 30, 2019.

Sincerely,

Rachel Dunnington
Registrar

1. Information about the organizing institution
   a. Contact names
   b. Address, with phone, mobile, e-mail
2. Venues to which exhibition will travel
3. Dates of the exhibition at each venue
4. Approximate travel dates
5. Specifications for transport
   a. All types: dual driver (nonsmokers), air-ride, climate-controlled vans
   b. High value: exclusive use, courier on board
   c. Medium value: exclusive use, or shared van with last-on, first-off
   d. Low value: shared van, shuttle
6. Crate list
   a. Numbers
   b. Dimensions
   c. Approximate weights
   d. List of extras/soft packs/furniture
7. Due date for estimate or bid

Confirmation Letter

After the shipping company is chosen, the organizer should provide a confirmation letter that states all pertinent information about the shipment and tour schedule, including names and contact information for representatives at each participating venue and notes about variations and exceptions that are planned to occur during the tour.

Sample Shipping Confirmation Letter

The ACME Fine Art Transport Company has been selected by The Sampler Museum to provide shipping services for the tour of the exhibition *Sample the Future*.

Confirmation Date: 15 March 2020

Organizer:
  The Sampler Museum
  123 Any Town Street
  Any Town, Any State, U.S.A.

  Rachel Dunnington, Registrar
  000-000-0001
  Mobile: 001-000-0000
  E-mail rdunnington@sample.org

The exhibition consists of 18 crates and 7 soft-packed panels.

Requirements for shipment for the US segments are:
  Exclusive-use van
  Dual drivers
  Air-ride
  Climate control, maintained at 70° F
  Lift gate

Exhibition Schedule and Contact Information

1. The Sampler Museum
   Any Town, Any State, U.S.A.
   September 26, 2020–January 2, 2021
2. The Bangor Museum
   Bangor, Maine
   February 3, 2021–May 23, 2021
     Contact: David Dell, Associate Registrar
     002-000-0000
     ddell@kearneyart.org
3. Sarasota History and Cultural Center
   Sarasota, Florida
   June 25, 2021–October 1, 2021
     Contact: Sydney Marsh, Curator
     003-000-0000
     smarsh@sarasotacenter.org

*October 10, 2021

Transport to Miami International Airport for shipment to Oslo, Norway. The panel packs will not travel to Oslo; they will return by shuttle to The Sampler Museum.

4. Oslo Technical Museum
   Oslo, Norway
   November 3, 2021–February 6, 2022
     Contact: Sylvia Teligman, Registrar
     011-004-000-0000
     sylviat@oslotech.nw

*February 15–20, 2022
Transport from Oslo Airport to Kennedy Airport, New York, then to the Sampler Museum for dispersal. Crate #16 will NOT be included in the final transport. It will be shipped directly to Italy by Oslo Transport.

Material to be shipped (length × depth × height)

Crate 1	80 × 30 × 55 in.
Crate 2	52 × 40 × 24 in.
Crate 3	90 × 15 × 60 in.
Crate 4	84 × 12 × 40 in.
Crate 5	50 × 32 × 30 in.
Crate 6	45 × 30 × 20 in.
Crate 7	32 × 32 × 24 in.
Crate 8	22 × 26 × 40 in.
Crate 9	22 × 26 × 40 in.
Crate 10	30 × 36 × 30 in.
Crate 11	42 × 30 × 12 in.
Crate 12	15 × 20 × 36 in.
Crate 13	30 × 30 × 20 in.
Crate 14	26 × 30 × 42 in.
Crate 15	24 × 36 × 24 in.
Crate 16	35 × 35 × 12 in.
Crate 17	35 × 35 × 12 in.
Crate 18	40 × 12 × 30 in.

Panel packs:
  4 @ 60 × 35 × 3 in.
  3 @ 52 × 40 × 3 in.

Proration of Tour Transportation Costs

[This is one method for prorating shipping costs, used by the Whitney Museum]

First, obtain estimates for round-trip transportation of the exhibition to each venue to know the amount that each venue would owe if they were the only stop on the tour.

Round-trip New York City to:

Toronto	$15,000
Miami	$25,000
San Francisco	$32,000
Montreal	$15,000
TOTAL:	**$87,000**

Using these figures, determine what percentage of the total transportation cost is owed by each venue.

Toronto	17.5%
Miami	28.5%
San Francisco	36.5%
Montreal	17.5%
TOTAL:	**100%**

Next, obtain a shipping estimate for the actual tour segments:

New York City to Toronto	$6,476.02
Toronto to Miami	$18,635.98
Miami to San Francisco	$18,397.43
San Francisco to Montreal	$20,805.02
Montreal to New York City	$8,658.04
TOTAL:	**$72,972.49**

Finally, using the percentages, determine the fair share of tour transportation costs owed by each exhibiting venue.

Toronto	$12,770.19
Miami	$20,797.16
San Francisco	$26,634.96
Montreal	$12,770.19
TOTAL:	**$72,972.50**

Everyone saves money; no one pays more than they would if they were the only venue. At the same time, no venue is subsidizing another.

Note: Add X% for fuel surcharge to each venue after final calculation.

5-3 CONDITION BOOKS

Checklist for Condition Book
1. Devise a numbering system for all objects in the exhibition.
2. Tag all objects with exhibition numbers.
3. Gather condition reports from lenders.
4. Gather photographs of all objects.
5. Check all condition report information and transfer it to a traveling report format.
   a. (Or add incoming reports to the condition book.)
6. Mark photographs with condition notes.
7. Place all reports, photographs, and notes in a three-ring binder.

The best format for a traveling exhibition's condition reports includes a clearly marked photograph of the object with notations about all areas that have or might have damage. Each object's condition report should include a description or a list of damaged areas and information about when and by whom the report was completed. At the beginning and end of each loan period, a responsible and knowledgeable individual—such as a curator, registrar, conservator, or preparator from the organizing institution or the exhibiting venue—should check every object against the incoming condition report and make appropriate notes on the report. "Unchanged" or "no change" is the optimal remark for the report at the end of the loan period, but any variations of condition, however small, should be noted. These annotations to the report should be signed and dated by the person performing the check.

The photograph and condition report are the most important object markers; together they form the key to risk management of the exhibition objects. It is important that any changes be reported to the registrar of record (i.e., the registrar named in the contract). If exhibitors do not have in-house conservators, the organizing registrar should contact conservators in the area and arrange for them to be on call to review damage and make repairs, if necessary.

A section of the condition book also can hold general reports on the photographic and interpretive panels that are sent with the exhibition. Upkeep of these panels must be figured into the time and cost for the exhibition.

1. DEVISE A NUMBERING SYSTEM FOR ALL OBJECTS IN THE EXHIBITION The exhibition's numbering system should correspond to the object's placement in the exhibition list, starting with 1. Ideally, this sequence will match the catalog number if a catalog accompanies the exhibition. If a problem occurs, make adjustments and write an explanation on the object list. As mentioned previously, to differentiate the exhibition number from the object's accession or temporary number, use a prefix. ("SF" for *Sample the Future* works as well here as it does for the crates.)

2. TAG ALL OBJECTS WITH EXHIBITION NUMBERS It has been the practice of many museums to put exhibition labels (with object identification information and exhibition number) on the backs of paintings and prints. Three-dimensional objects, however, should not be marked in any way, even temporarily. An acid-free tag placed in a bag, attached to a wire or a mount, or placed in a box with the object should be used to identify the object when it is not on display.

3. GATHER CONDITION REPORTS FROM LENDERS Initial condition reports, completed when the objects leave their owners, should be supplemented and reworked into a single format that will be used for the traveling portion of the exhibition. Use the initial condition reports to check information and ensure that everything has been noted.

4. GATHER PHOTOGRAPHS OF ALL OBJECTS If objects have been photographed for the catalog, cut up a copy and use the images in the condition book. The better the quality of the photograph, the easier, safer, and more efficient condition reporting will be. Use one of the following (listed in order of quality): a color photograph (or photographs, for three-dimensional objects), catalog pages, black-and-white photographs, or copies of photographs. Digital technology makes it fairly simple to take a good quality photograph and print it on a color printer.

5. CHECK ALL CONDITION REPORT INFORMATION AND TRANSFER IT TO A TRAVELING REPORT FORMAT Make a condition report for each object as it comes in. Prepare the traveling format and use it, as the objects in the exhibition are examined. A second report will be done when the exhibition travels, but it is best for the organizing museum to have as much as possible ready before it deinstalls the exhibition.

6. MARK PHOTOGRAPHS WITH CONDITION NOTES Circle or point to all areas of concern on the photograph, and write on it clearly. If it is not possible to write directly on the photograph, put it in a Mylar sleeve and write on the sleeve with a permanent marker.

7. PLACE ALL REPORTS, PHOTOGRAPHS, AND NOTES INTO A THREE-RING BINDER Three-ring binders remain the condition report books of choice. Organize them clearly by exhibition number, or exhibition section, if applicable, and ensure that each report clearly shows object's information, owner, and numbers.

Digital Condition Reporting

by Jacqueline Cabrera
formerly of the J. Paul Getty Museum

When the iPad made its debut on April 3, 2010, the world of the registrar and condition reporting began to move to another level of efficiency and accessibility. However, because many cultural institutions have not upgraded their on-site Internet servers to the point where galleries have accessible or, more importantly, reliable Wi-Fi, the traditional hard copy condition report binder has not completely disappeared. Therefore, before moving to digital condition reporting, speak to your museum's information technology (IT) specialist to be sure the system will support integrating a tablet into your daily tasks or exhibition loans.

Using digital reports instead of hard copies offers several advantages. See sample digital report, pp. 53–54. Digital reports are easy to mark up, add photos, and share via e-mail or through a shared data file server, such as Dropbox or Box.com. They can remain editable to allow your counterpart registrar to make additions as needed throughout the run of a loan. They also do not take up much room—just the size of a tablet, as opposed to one or two three-inch binders in your suitcase.

Here are guidelines I recommend for the use of a tablet in creating digital condition reports on incoming exhibition loans:

1. Use application programs that are inexpensive and are from well-known application providers. It will be easier to get customer support when needed, 24/7, no matter where you are in the world. I use basic MS Word to prepare the template and the app PDF Expert to mark up the report as I check the condition of the object.

2. When you travel with an exhibition, make sure the contract includes wording about gallery Wi-Fi needs. It is disheartening to arrive at a museum and find out their server cannot accommodate your digital reports, forcing you to revert to the condition report binder. Imagine if you neglected to prepare one!

3. Images can say more than words, so take many photographs when preparing the report. However, to keep your report at a manageable size, only attach the images of problem areas to your report. Retain the other images in a folder on your computer.

4. Make sure to mark the photographs with text or arrows clearly indicating the problem area(s). Make sure to date your comments, especially for objects in traveling exhibitions, to pinpoint when and where the problem was noted.

5. When preparing the report template make sure the cover page includes basic object data, along with exhibition title and display dates and a clear image of the object. If the loan is going to a single venue, add signature lines at the bottom of the front page, with room for comments as needed.

6. If the loan will travel to multiple venues, leave an entire page (ideally page 2) where representatives of each venue can sign and provide comments as needed. I have seen many reports where space was not allocated for future use. The result is a PDF with signatures and comments fit into any available space all over the report.

7. My reports are usually about four to five pages long. A report for a three-dimensional object, should have an extra page to accommodate photographs from many different angles.

   - First page: object data and image, with problem areas indicated or described.
   - Second page, multiple venues: additional signatures and comments for each venue.
   - Third to fifth pages: annotated detail images added to the report. Always leave the last page blank so that future users can add images as needed.

8. When adding comments to an existing digital report, keep the font at a reasonable reading size. I find 10 point works well, is legible, and does not require too much space on the page. In addition, make sure your electronic signature is the same size as your font. Be consistent when adding comments. I like to mark my notes as follows:

   2/25/19: No changes <signature>
   5/19/19: Additional scratches noted; refer to photographs; otherwise, no other changes <signature>

9. Keep the process simple. Here is how I create my own reports.

   a. I prepare a template using MS Word.
   b. I then save it as a PDF file.
   c. I save the PDF file on a shared file server such as Box .com or Dropbox.
   d. Using the PDF Expert application on my iPad, I access the file via this shared file server.
   e. I add photos, make edits, and add my signature as needed. I then save the file in the same folder.
   f. I give my counterpart registrar access to the folder, making sure to include permission to edit, so he or she can use the reports as needed throughout the duration of the loan.

Extra tip: I like to edit images via the iPad's photo app, which makes it easy to crop the photo and add arrows and comments. I save the image and then add it to the report via PDF Expert.

In general, keep digital reports simple. Images speak louder than words and provide a much clearer idea of the problem areas than do words.

The iPad can also be used during installation or deinstallation for marking checklists and signing incoming and outgoing receipts or shipping receipts. These forms can be e-mailed to your colleagues via the PDF Expert application while you are still in the gallery! Simple and efficient.

THE SAMPLER MUSEUM

SAMPLE THE FUTURE!

Checklist #29

Crate # 8

Gander Monton, American, b. 1968
Found in Space I, 1998
Computer-generated prints, each 22 x 28 in.   Framed 23 x 29 in.
Lent by the artist

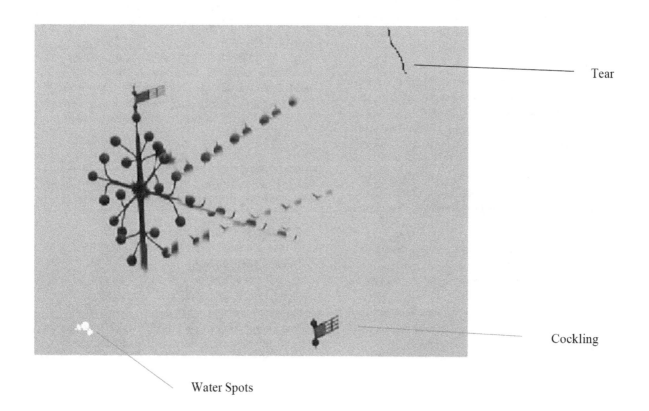

Tear

Cockling

Water Spots

✓ Fading overall
✓ Cockling, most pronounced on right side
✓ Repaired tear, upper right, 1 in. from corner, 1 in. in length
✓ Small water spots, lower left corner

Silver-colored metal frame has abrasions along right side, slight separation of miter in upper right corner.

Sample manual condition report, including pages for recording incoming and outgoing condition checks at each tour venue.

THE SAMPLER MUSEUM

SAMPLE THE FUTURE!

Checklist #29   *Crate # 8*

Gander Monton, American, b. 1968
Found in Space I, 1998
Computer-generated prints, each 22 x 28 in.   Framed 23 x 29 in.
Lent by the artist

Venue 1: Sampler Museum   September 26, 2020 – January 2, 2021
Incoming Condition:

Signature: Date:

Outgoing Condition:

Signature: Date:

Venue 2: The Bangor Museum   February 3, 2021 – 21 May 23, 2020
Incoming Condition:

Signature: Date:

Outgoing Condition:

Signature: Date:

SAMPLE THE FUTURE!

Checklist #29   *Crate # 8*

Gander Monton, American, b. 1968
Found in Space I, 1998
Computer-generated prints, each 22 x 28 in.   Framed 23 x 29 in.
Lent by the artist

Venue 3: Sarasota History and Cultural Center   June 25, 2020 – October 1, 2020
Incoming Condition:

Signature: Date:

Outgoing Condition:

Signature: Date:

Venue 4: Oslo Technical Museum   November 3, 2020 – February 6, 2021
Incoming Condition:

Signature: Date:

Outgoing Condition:

Signature: Date:

SAMPLE DIGITAL CONDITION REPORT

CABRERA + ART + MANAGEMENT   Condition Report

Artist: Unknown
Object Title: Shaker Box
Medium: wood   Date: 2010
Dimensions (H x W x L in.): Lid: H 1 ½ x dia. 6 in.; Box: H 3 x dia. 5 7/8 in.
Inventory number: JMC.001
Lender: Private Collection, Los Angeles, CA, USA

Preexisting condition:

Structure/Frame: ☐ Stable   ☐ Unstable

☐ Visible cracks   ☐ Soiling
☐ Unfilled losses   ☐ Grime
☐ Stains/residue   ☐ Split
☐ Localized abrasions   ☐ Glazed
☐ Scratches/gouges   ☐ Acrylic

Artwork: ☑ Stable   ☐ Unstable

☑ Abrasion   ☐ Foxing
☐ Cockling   ☐ Mold/Mildew
☐ Gouge   ☐ Soil
☐ Discoloration   ☑ Grime
☐ Fading   ☐ Tear
☐ Flake   ☐ Crease

Additional notes:

> Overall in good condition. Minor scratches noted. A small surface loss is noted on the side of the bottom section.
>
> Refer to additional notes on additional pages. Refer to images provided with this report.

Condition report provided by Lender: ☑ No   ☐ Yes

Incoming: Outgoing:

Check by: _____JMC_____   Check by: _____

Date: _____3/30/19_____   Date: _____

Sample digital condition report produced from an iPad.
Courtesy of Jacqueline Cabrera, formerly of the J. Paul Getty Museum.

Additional notes/photograph:

Scratches noted

Surface loss

Courtesy of Jacqueline Cabrera, formerly of the J. Paul Getty Museum.

5-4 DESIGN ELEMENTS

Checklist for Label and Panel Production
1. Curator writes label.
2. Label and panel text goes through institutional editing process.
3. Exhibition department creates digital copy.
4. Exhibition department produces hard copy.

Labels
The organizer can send finished labels to each venue. It is more common, however, to send digital information so the exhibitor can format and produce its own labels on the paper stock and in the color of its own choice. It is usual, too, for exhibitors' designers to visit the exhibition at a previous site before it arrives at their institutions. Relevant details of design, potential problems, and appropriate solutions then can be discussed with the staff of the organizing institution.

Panels
Interpretive panels often travel with an exhibition. They may be stand-alone panels or panels that can be mounted on a wall. As with label copy, it is best to provide panel information in a digital format so that the borrowing institutions can make changes in the design or method of presentation. Photographic panels commonly travel with exhibitions and should have their own section in the condition report book so that information about wear and needed replacement is easily accessible.

Audio/Video
Exhibitions may have audio and video components traveling with them; these often will have tapes, CDs, and DVDs that are part of the program. To ensure that the programs can be played without interruption, the organizing institution should keep a backup machine

ready for overnight shipment, particularly if a special type of audio or video unit is used. It is also a good idea to provide all specifications for the equipment traveling with the exhibition as well as information about where to acquire repairs and replacements. Providing such information is particularly important when the audio or video is part of an object and, therefore, likely to need an exact replacement (e.g., an object with several video monitors that all look alike). If generic equipment, such as a standard VCR or DVD player, is used, such measures are not as necessary.

Tapes should be duplicated and several copies sent with the exhibition. Although DVDs are more stable, they also should have backups. All of these items should be added to the appropriate crate lists.

Samples

Educational, hands-on, or try-on material incorporated in an exhibition should be clearly designated as such and accompanied by information about which mounts are necessary or recommended. For example, an exhibition on weaving may include samples that can be touched by the audience. Attaching them firmly to a board and providing mounting instructions will help the exhibitor understand exactly how they should be viewed and used. List samples in the condition book, and indicate whether condition reports are necessary or if any object that becomes seriously damaged, worn, or soiled should be replaced. Extra samples should be kept by the organizing institution for use in such cases.

Furniture/Mounts

Exhibition pedestals rarely are included in a traveling exhibition. Shipping pedestals can be cost-prohibitive; adding them to the shipping list soon leads to a second truck and double the transportation costs. In addition, they damage easily; pedestals included in a show toured by Smithsonian Institution Traveling Exhibition Service (SITES), for example, had to be protected by custom-fitted blanket wraps. Vitrines also break easily and must be protected in transit and handling.

Both case furniture and mounts can be designed for travel. There are several points to note about mounts. If an exhibitor uses new colors and installs its own pedestals and vitrines, it may be difficult for the organizer's mount to blend in. In such cases, the organizer can permit the painting of mounts. If the show is being installed exactly as (or as close as possible to) the original installation, however, sending mounts may save

the exhibitor valuable time. The traveling exhibition coordinator should work out these details between the originating and borrowing venues.

If an exhibition contains a number of large textiles, it makes sense to send along acid-free tubes in which to store them and mounts with which to install them. If specific microenvironments are required, it is important that the mounts be designed to travel from venue to venue. Again, the most important thing is communication. Organizing and borrowing institutions must stay in close communication during the exhibition to ensure that all goes smoothly.

Design Book

A design book can simplify even the most difficult installation. The organizing institution should produce such a book and send it to all participating venues. Among the details that should comprise a design book are the following:

1. contact information for the organizing designer
2. object photographs (in color if possible), in exhibition order
3. object information (To this point, the design book and condition book are the same and can be produced at the same time.)
   a. notes on mounting for difficult objects
   b. notes on objects that need rigging
   c. notes on objects that will be accompanied by couriers
4. layout of first-site exhibition with numbers (or better yet, pictures) showing the installation of objects
5. manufacturer's number for paint color and color swatches for all areas of the exhibition
6. a list of mounts, furniture, and cases that will be sent with the exhibition
7. information on labels and panels that will be sent with the exhibition

Catalogs and Sale Objects

The organizer's shop manager and the exhibitor's shop manager should review the kinds of exhibition-related materials that will be available for sale. Some of the complimentary catalogs sent with the show will go to the shop, after the curator, registrar, administration, and development offices receive their copies. At some museums the shop manager receives all merchandise associated with an exhibition and gives copies of catalogs to the appropriate staff. At other institutions the project manager receives and distributes catalogs.

Education Programs and Packets

The traveling exhibitions coordinator should receive copies of educational handouts, as well as notes on all programs produced for the exhibition, and use them to create an educational packet for the borrowing institution. Each exhibitor likely will want to produce its own educational programs, but the base material will be beneficial. The exhibitor's educator often travels with the designer to see a prior installation of the exhibition before producing local programming. A mainstay for docent training is to have the organizer's curator speak at the exhibition's opening and provide training for docents during his or her visit.

DISPLAY NOTES

Mounting/ Hanging device: ☐ Cleats ☐ D-rings ☐ Oz clips ☐ Mount ☐ No Mounting Support Needed
Notes/Description:

Page 5 of a Mint Museum electronic condition report showing installation notes.
Photograph by Brandon Scott.

5-5 TRAVELING PERSONNEL

Exhibition Couriers

The decision to require a courier or couriers for traveling exhibitions is based on several criteria: difficulty of installation, valuation of objects, and fragility of objects. Staff members from the organizing institution, as well as staff from lending individuals or institutions, may be required to be on-site at the venue when the exhibition is installed or deinstalled. Simple and low-value exhibitions may travel without couriers or installers. A representative of the organizer will generally travel to venues if an exhibition is complex or of high value. A courier or couriers from one or more lenders may travel with an exhibition between venues, as well. In some cases, a curator will travel to the borrowing institution to speak at the opening, at a symposium, or at docent training. Directors and other administrators sometimes also travel to opening events. It should be understood that these other personnel, if not also acting as courier, have different roles.

The classic museum courier, as described by Cordelia Rose in her book *Courierspeak*, is able to "make condition reports, photograph, handle, pack and unpack objects, oversee transport and stay with the shipment to its final destination, make insurance documentation, install and, in some cases, repair or remount an object." The traveling exhibition courier may do some or all of these tasks. The traveling exhibition courier is responsible for oversight of the exhibition at all points and is the representative of the organizer's institution while fulfilling these duties.

There are often broader expectations for the staff member or consultant who travels to oversee an installation. In addition to acting as a true courier, he or she may also answer questions about publicity, education packets, label content and production, design, credit lines, and catalogs along with the condition reports, crating decisions, and intricate aspects of installation. In all cases, he or she serves as a liaison between the organizer and the venue and finds answers to all questions that arise. In lieu of a traveling staff member, the organizer's coordinator for the exhibition may send an information overview notebook with the condition reports, exhibition/installation requirements, and design books. It is important that the organizer stay in close touch with the venue's project coordinator.

The organizing institution should define the roles of the personnel traveling with an exhibition and make it clear in advance which jobs will be the responsibility of the venue and which will be managed by the organizer. A well-crafted contract is the vehicle by which

such roles are clarified. (See chapter 4 for a discussion of contracts.) The organizer's courier might travel with the crates, oversee the loading dock activity, be present for unpacking and condition reporting, and possibly oversee installation. There is often, however, a time gap between the arrival of the exhibition and its installation, so it may be necessary to decide what is most important: to travel with the exhibition or to oversee the installation. Or it may be necessary to send someone for both time periods. The decisions must be based on the fragility and value of the objects, the difficulty of the transit, the complexity of the installation, the size of the exhibition, and the time line that has been established.

Some museums with an extensive traveling exhibitions program have created a coordinator or manager of traveling exhibitions position. The coordinator may be the one who travels to the borrowing venue, and if so, is familiar with all aspects of the exhibition as well as the needs of the objects.

- The organizer works with the venue to determine the courier's schedule.
- The venue usually is responsible for making travel and hotel arrangements for the courier, although expenses are paid by the organizer.
- The exhibition courier will generally be paid per diem travel expenses by the organizer, which are factored into the exhibition fee paid by the venues.
- The courier's jobs may include traveling with the exhibition, unpacking, condition reporting, and installing the exhibition. Details of the courier's responsibilities should be made clear to the venue in the exhibition contract.

Loan Courier

If the exhibition is made up of objects borrowed from various lenders, individual lenders may require that their representatives accompany and monitor their loans. Loan couriers may bring the loaned objects to the first venue and return at the end of the exhibition to retrieve those objects; in some cases, the courier will also return to travel with the objects between venues. These couriers fit the definition of the classic couriers. They will travel with the work, unpack and condition report at the destination, and, in many cases, install the objects.

Courier schedules are vital to the smooth installation of the exhibition. One or two couriers may be easily integrated into a schedule. Fifteen or twenty make the initial installation a special challenge but

I was on a truck from Philadelphia to Fort Worth. We had stopped at a big truck stop in Knoxville, Tennessee, around 1 AM. The drivers went in to take a break, and I stayed with the truck. While waiting, I saw a rig trying to back into a parking space. He rammed into the trailer of another semi, then pulled back out, and left. The truck he hit didn't seem damaged, but it was enough of a hit that the trailer was still rocking and the load could have shifted. This brought home to me one reason why we require couriers on exhibition trucks and why the courier makes sure that the truck is never left unattended. If that incident had happened with an art hauler, the crates could have shifted, straps could have pulled out, loose crates might be moving around in the trailer, and the drivers would have no idea that anything was wrong. A serious chance for damage.

—Randy Cleaver, formerly Philadelphia Museum of Art

are often the norm, especially with three-dimensional object exhibitions.

- Schedule courier arrivals at intervals, avoiding weekend travel when possible.
- If it is possible to accommodate several couriers at one time, consolidate shipments to save money.
- Leave a 24-hour window for acclimatization of crates, more if a lender demands more.
- Schedule intervals for unpacking and condition reporting based on the complexity of the object and its installation. Or coordinate, if necessary, to complete a case or platform installation with multiple lenders' objects.

It is standard practice for transportation and lodging arrangements for a lender's courier to be arranged by the venue; payment for courier travel and per diem allowance will be borne by the organizer as established in the exhibition contract. Some couriers may prefer to make their own travel arrangements, but the cost is borne by the organizer. The venue should provide the courier with details and confirmations of all travel arrangements.

It is also standard for courier trips to be three days and two nights for domestic shipments in the United States, four days and three nights for European trips. Longer time periods are necessary for Australia and Asia and for difficult travel destinations. Per diem amount is determined by costs at the destination of the courier as well as current market costs, although some lenders may dictate the per diem that must be paid to their couriers. In 2019, for example, a courier in the

New York City area receives a per diem of $75–$100, plus local travel of $100. The per diem is not taxable, and it is unnecessary to get a courier's Social Security number. The money is to be spent for food, incidentals, and all local transportation.

Checklist for Courier Care

1. Make travel arrangements for the lender's courier. Usually a courier travels economy class on the leg of the trip without the object but business class when accompanying the object. Business class should always be used for hand-carried objects, and lenders often request business class on both legs of exceptionally long trips, as well. At times, economics may dictate that one type of flight is much less costly than another.
2. Book accommodations for the courier. It is usual to pay only for the basic room with applicable taxes; food, telephone, and other incidentals are paid by the courier from the per diem. Be certain that the courier is aware of this situation and that he or she makes arrangements to have a credit card or cash and phone card available.
3. Provide the courier with an information sheet before he or she travels.
4. When the courier is traveling with objects, be certain that the courier is officially met at the arrival point, if by air (most often done by an agent) or at the loading dock, if arriving by truck.
5. Secure the arriving works in safe storage with the courier present.
6. Provide the courier with a welcome packet that includes information about the museum, local transportation, restaurants, and activities.
7. Include the total per diem payment in cash in the packet, along with a receipt to be signed and returned. It is best that this transaction take place as soon after the courier arrives as practical. If the courier travels separately from the shipment, arrange to have the packet and per diem waiting at the hotel or have an agent meet the courier when he or she arrives to turn over the packet and accept the signed receipt.
8. If possible, assure that local transport is available to the courier on arrival and schedule unpacking and condition inspection at least 24 hours after arrival.
9. Once an object is unpacked, condition reports are completed and agreed on, installation is done, and all receipts are countersigned, the responsibility of the courier is finished.

Template for Confirming Courier Information

[Note: << >> indicates typical field names for data that can be drawn from the exhibition database.]

Sample the Future THE SAMPLER MUSEUM 123 Any Street, Any Town, Any State 00000 Contact: Rachel Dunnington, Registrar; Telephone: 000-000-0001

COURIER INFORMATION

Courier Name:	«Courier_First_Name» «Courier_Last_Name»
Institution:	«Institution»
Phone:	<<Courier_phone>>
Mobile:	«Fax»
E-mail:	«Email»
Loans:	«Artist_First_Name» «Artist_Last_Name», «Object_Title», «Medium», «Date»
Sampler Arrival Date:	«Newark_Arrival_Date» «Newark_Arrival_Notes»

HOTEL INFORMATION:

Hotel:	<<hotel_name>> <<hotel_address>>
Telephone:	<<hotel_phone>>
Website/E-mail:	<<hotel_website>>, <<hotel_email>>
Hotel Dates:	«Hotel_Dates»
Hotel Confirmation #:	«Hotel_Confirmation»

MUSEUM INFORMATION:

Name and Address:	The Sampler Museum 123 Any Street Any Town, Any State 00000
Museum Contact:	<<Contact_name>>
Contact Phone:	<<Contact_mobile>>
Museum Arrival:	«UnpackInstall_Sampler»
Arrival Instructions:	Enter at the North Wing entrance to The Sampler Museum (on right of driveway from Any Street, green doors). Ask Security to call the Registrar.
Per Diem:	«Per_Diem_amt»
	(Your per diem will be given to you at the time of arrival at the Sampler Museum or at the hotel.)

CONTACT INFORMATION:
If you have questions about this Information Sheet, please contact:
- Rachel Dunnington, Registrar, The Sampler Museum
  Telephone: 000-000-0001   rdunnington@sampler.org
- 24-Hour Security Desk at The Sampler Museum (for late night arrivals)
  Telephone: 000-000-0009

TRAVEL INFORMATION

Travel Directions to High Class Hill Hotel from the local airports
BEST OPTION: High Class Hill Hotel Courtesy Shuttle, which picks up from Any Town International Airport. The shuttle is complimentary; however, it is customary to tip the driver $1 or $2 per ride and $1 per piece of luggage.

1. Pick up your luggage
2. Go to Monorail Station E. (You will see people in red coats.)
3. Pick up a courtesy phone and dial #11 for the High Class Hill Hotel.
4. Hotel staff will tell you if a shuttle is already on its way to the airport or will send one to pick you up.

Driving directions from Any Town International Airport to High Class Hill Hotel:
  Distance from hotel: 13 mi.
  From airport, take route 10 to route 22, which will become Anywhere Highway. Proceed down Anywhere Highway North for 2.5 miles. Make a right-hand turn onto Market Street. At the next light make a left turn onto 3rd Street. The hotel is on the left.

Taxi: Typical minimum charge from the airport is USD 21.00

For couriers arriving on a truck: If you arrive with an art shipment, you will enter The Sampler Museum at the loading dock, near the parking lot. Walk up the ramp on the garden side to get to the door. Use the telephone by the door to call the Security Desk.

Travel Directions from the High Class Hill Hotel to The Samper Museum

Best Option: High Class Hill Hotel Courtesy Shuttle, which takes hotel residents to and from the museum or other local destinations and the hotel. The shuttle is complimentary; just tip the driver $1 or $2 per ride. Call 000-000-5000 to make a reservation.

Walking/Driving Directions from the High Class Hill Hotel to The Sampler Museum. Allow 15–20 minutes for walking, 10 minutes for driving.

1. From the front of the hotel, head west on 3rd Street (left from hotel's main entrance). Go six blocks to Any Street.
2. Turn right on Any Street. Go five blocks.
3. Enter at the north doors.

Public Transportation:
   Buses #13 and #27 run from 3rd Street Station stop near the Museum, located at 3rd and Any Place, to a stop near the hotel's side entrance. Cash required for fare. For additional bus information, call 1-800-000-RIDE, or ask the concierge at the hotel.

Taxi Cab Companies:
   Green Taxi, 000-000-4000. It is best to ask the concierge at the hotel to call a taxi for you. The drive to the museum takes about 15 minutes, but allow additional time for the taxi to arrive at the hotel and the Museum.

We look forward to meeting you and receiving the objects for this important exhibition.

Best regards,

Rachel Dunnington, Registrar
The Sampler Museum

cc: Shipping Company

THE SAMPLER MUSEUM [letterhead]

Courier Per Diem Receipt

Exhibition:	*Sample the Future*
Venue:	The Sampler Museum
Dates:	26 September 2020–2 January 2021

The Sampler Museum agrees to make per diem payments to couriers accompanying loans to the venue listed above for the exhibition, *Sample the Future*, to cover costs of food, local transportation, and incidentals.

I, _____ (signature), understand that it is my responsibility to pay for the aforementioned items and that I will not be reimbursed for these costs in any further way. I hereby acknowledge receipt of the per diem amount as follows.

Courier name:

Courier address:

Lender:

Object:

Per diem cash received:

Date:

Please sign both copies and return one copy to The Sampler Museum

5-6 THE FIRST VENUE ON THE ROAD

Most of the problems surrounding the logistics of the traveling exhibition will happen at the first venue. Therefore, the organizing institution's curator and registrar must talk to their counterparts at the first venue well in advance of the shipment of objects and educational packets, going over all of the dates, the need (if applicable) for couriers, the publications, and other details that come up. The conversation may be quick or involved, depending on the complexity of the exhibition. The exhibitor's designer should have visited the

exhibition already and will probably have much to ask the organizing curator and designer about the details of the exhibition to ensure that the same story will be told in a different space.

The sequence is fairly simple. The exhibitor's design and exhibition construction staff have a two- to three-month schedule for case and special construction; they work to bring together everything they will need to install the exhibition in the three- to four-week window usually allowed for exhibition change. The exhibitor's registrar informs operations personnel about special delivery or security needs and works with the originating registrar to determine shipping dates and make arrangements for accommodations and per diem payments for couriers from lenders.

When the shipment arrives at the first venue, it is taken to the designated exhibition preparation area. Because space allocation in most museums does not allow for real exhibition preparation rooms—where objects might be brought in, uncrated, condition reported, and set up for installation—the preparation area often is the closed gallery where the new exhibition eventually will be on view. There is always an acclimatization period of 24 to 48 hours. The originating institution will tell the exhibitor exactly how long the acclimatization period should be.

If the originating institution has decided to send a courier with the exhibition, that person helps with the unpacking, condition reporting, and installation, solving problems as they arise and working through the usual details of an installation. If there is no courier, the exhibitor's registrar will unpack and condition report the objects, and the installation staff at that museum will install everything according to the organizer's written instructions. If lenders send their own couriers, a separate schedule for unpacking and installation should be set up for their objects; usually, these items are installed closest to the opening of the exhibition. As problems arise, they can be worked out in meetings and discussions among the exhibitor's staff or by working with the organizing institution.

Then the exhibition will be off and running, usually with minimal scares and nightmares. Advance preparation and care of the details will make it work.

CHAPTER 6

Upkeep

Once an exhibition is on the road, it soon disappears from the minds of most staff at the organizing museum. The coordinator of traveling exhibitions must be the exception. It is up to him or her to make certain that other staff continue their work to maintain the exhibition and ensure that its installation at each venue proceeds smoothly.

6-1 COURIERS

It is decidedly easier to take care of a traveling exhibition if the organizing institution sends a staff member to each venue, first to oversee unpacking, condition reporting, and installation and then again to deinstall, condition report, pack, and send the exhibition to the next venue. The decision about whether to assign a registrar or a traveling exhibitions coordinator generally is based on the complexity, value, and financial health of the exhibition. (See also "Traveling Personnel" in chapter 5.)

As the organizer's representative travels from site to site, he or she can monitor exhibition materials and help rotate objects in and out of the show, if necessary. Having a representative on-site allows the organizing institution to provide an immediate response when problems arise and takes away much of the responsibility from the exhibitor's staff. If there is no representative, the organizer should devise a satisfactory way to monitor the exhibition, provide replacements, and solve problems. That can be accomplished in part by requesting condition reports from the participating venues and scheduling regular discussions with their staff. If a curatorial lecturer or other staff member visits the exhibitor for a program or event, that person can be asked to review the materials. But even if the organizer does not send a representative to each venue for installation and deinstallation, it at least should send someone for a day or two to review the exhibition at its second or third venue.

6-2 CONTACTS BETWEEN THE EXHIBITING AND ORGANIZING INSTITUTIONS

Regular communication is the best possible way to ensure the success of an exhibition's installation and its ongoing programs. The curator of the exhibition at the organizing institution will talk with the exhibitor's designated contact about lectures and docent training. The registrars will discuss shipment dates, couriers, restriction notes, packing notes, and security issues. The organizing designer of the exhibition will be asked to explain the mounts and other design issues.

Most communication between other functional areas of the museums, and perhaps even some of what has already been discussed, will be done through the traveling exhibition coordinator. Such communication might focus on questions about publicity, photographs, museum shop items, catalogs, and educational programs, which often arise during the run of a show.

6-3 CONTACTS WITH LENDERS

During the run of an exhibition there will be times when the organizing museum must be in touch with the lenders to the show. For example, some lenders will request periodic updates on condition reports or, as noted previously, will ask that their couriers be present when their loans are installed and deinstalled.

6-4 SCHEDULE CHANGES

Exhibitors must notify both lenders and the organizing institution about changes to the exhibition schedule. Minor changes, such as new opening dates, often are sent as a courtesy. However, if there are major changes, such as anything that entails movement or storage beyond the scope of the contract or withdrawal of an exhibiting venue, lenders must be contacted. All changes of venue must be approved by the lenders.

6-5 INCIDENTS

The organizing museum is responsible for contacting the lender if there is a physical problem with a loaned object or if changes must be made to mounts or frames. If damage occurs to an object, the owner must be contacted before conservation begins, unless immediate treatment is necessary to pervert further loss or damage. Incidents may happen during shipping, unpacking, installation, or exhibition; the contract should outline the procedure the exhibitor must follow to report an incident to the organizer immediately. The organizer's registrar will report the problem to the lender and obtain authorization to respond.

Essential information documenting incidents includes:

- photographs of the object and details of the area where damage occurred
- numbers and descriptions of all objects involved
- identification of the place where the incident occurred
- statements from people who witnessed the incident, if applicable
- description of the incident
- notes about actions taken
- name of person reporting the incident
- date of report

If damage occurs to exhibition objects or materials, the organizing institution should help replace the items or repair the damage.

6-6 ROTATION OF SENSITIVE MATERIALS

Several categories of objects can be shown at only one or two venues:

- Works on paper
- Textiles
- Objects that are too fragile for extended travel
- Objects that are on short-term loan

Light damage to works on paper and textiles is cumulative. Thus, such items should be shown for restricted amounts of time because nothing will restore them; once a color fades, it is lost forever. To slow damage, institutions limit the amount of time an object can be exhibited and the amount of light that can be used to highlight it. Textiles and works on paper, particularly watercolors, often are restricted to five to eight foot-candles.

The curatorial staff is charged with finding enough strong and thematic objects or artworks to make the necessary changes possible. The registrar arranges to ship rotating objects to and from the proper venues, apart from the main shipments that are made.

6-7 INVOICES AND PAYMENTS

Establishing invoice and payment schedules for traveling exhibitions is simple, but it is crucial that someone keep focus on invoices and payments at all times. Because the billing process is drawn out over a long period of time, it is easy to lose track if everything is not recorded and there is no follow-through.

The Exhibition Fee Tracking Form will help museums monitor invoices and payments.

Exhibition Fee Tracking Form

	Venue 1	*Venue 2*	*Venue 3*	*Venue 4*
Venue Name				
Contact				
Phone				
Mobile				
E-mail				
Exhibition fee invoice 1 sent				
Exhibition fee invoice 1 paid				
Shipment invoice 1 sent				
Shipment invoice 1 paid				
Shipment invoice 2 sent				
Shipment invoice 2 paid				
Shipment invoice 3 sent				
Shipment invoice 3 paid				
Adjustment billed or paid*				

*For prorated shipping

CHAPTER 7

The Last Stop on the Tour: Dispersal

The last step in managing a traveling exhibition is dispersal: returning all objects to their accustomed locations, tying up loose ends, and recording information for future reference.

7-1 RETURNS

If the exhibition is composed entirely of objects from the organizer's collection, returns are simple. The exhibition can, in that case, be returned to the organizer by the same shipping method used for transfers between venues. This transit was likely incorporated into the original shipping request for proposal (RFP), and the only arrangement to be completed is scheduling. Communication is again crucial in selecting a shipping schedule that allows the staff at the final venue time to pack, fits into the transporter's workload, and deposits the exhibition on the organizer's loading dock at a convenient time.

An exhibition containing loan materials has more options for dispersal and requires more complex planning. It is possible, of course, to return the exhibition intact to the organizer and stage returns to lenders from there, as for any other exhibition composed of loaned materials. In many cases, however, it will be preferable to disperse some or all of the loans from the final venue.

Checklist for Deciding Whether to Disperse from Final Venue or from Organizer's Location

1. Can the organizer send someone to perform outgoing condition checks at the final venue?
2. Will there be one or more couriers from lenders to oversee crating and shipping of individual objects?
3. Do any of the objects have to be removed from travel crates and wrapped or recrated in original containers before return to owners?
4. Is the staff at the last venue able and willing to oversee individual shipments from their site?
5. Are destinations of returns closer to the last venue or to the organizer?

To decide how to organize returns, first consider whether a courier can be sent to the last venue to complete final condition reports. It is important that someone from the organizing institution—the borrower of record of objects in the exhibition—check each work to determine what, if any, changes have occurred during the course of the traveling exhibition. If a representative of the organizer cannot go to the final venue to make this examination, it may be necessary to return the exhibition to home base to do so. The cost of sending a courier should be weighed against the time and effort required to uncrate the exhibition, check condition, and recrate for return to owners.

Returns that must be supervised or accompanied by a courier from the lender will likely be made from the final venue. Such special arrangements should be made as far in advance as possible to clarify the situation for the remaining objects.

Crating considerations also enter into the decision about where to stage the dispersal. If all objects belonging to a single lender are individually crated

---

Scene: Planeside in Newark (back in the days when you could go planeside) with a shipment I've just couriered from a lender on the West Coast. I'm in a van following my two containers that are on the end of the "train" of containers. In front of my two containers are two others, both in the distinct form of an insulated container transporting human remains. Suddenly, the last four containers (mine and the two coffin-shaped ones) begin to wag back and forth until the momentum detaches them from the lead car! I watch in horror as they race straight for and crash through the cyclone fence! I spend helpless hours on the tarmac waiting (in 90-degree heat, as I recall) for airport security to come repair the breach in the security barrier (higher priority to them than getting me to the cargo facility) before finally being brought, with my cargo intact, to the shed. Nothing damaged. Well, I don't know about the contents of those other two containers!

—Maureen McCormick, formerly
Princeton Art Museum, Princeton, New Jersey

or crated only with each other, returns from the final venue are possible. However, if works received soft wrap or were removed from original shipping containers and were combined with other loans or permanent collection items, it will probably be easier to return them to the organizer's location to restore them to original shipping status. It is possible, as well, to split the shipments, sending part of the exhibition back to the organizing institution and dispersing part of it from the final venue.

The cooperation of the final venue is an essential element in deciding how to accomplish exhibition dispersal. If staff availability, skill, time, and willingness to oversee individual shipments from their location do not exist, it will not be possible to stage returns from the final venue.

Finally, the destination of returns, relative to the locations of the organizer and final venue, influences dispersal decisions. A list of loans by location should illustrate whether to disperse from the final venue or from the organizer's home. For example, a final venue on the West Coast but organizer and lenders in the Midwest and East would make it more sensible to take them home for dispersal. On the other hand, an organizer located in an extreme corner of the country, Florida or Maine, perhaps, likely would find it more economical and desirable to make returns from a centrally located final venue. In all likelihood, the organizer will decide on a combination of return arrangements: Those returns that are closer to the final venue will be dispersed from there, and those closer to the organizer or requiring removal from travel crates will return to home base for dispersal.

Once the decision about returns is made, the process is the same as for consolidation:

1. Unless there was an understanding with a particular carrier to provide all shipping for the exhibition, repeat the RFP for shippers. If dispersal was included in a comprehensive original RFP, it may not be necessary to repeat it; however, the possibility of changing needs and circumstances, particularly with a long tour, make it preferable to request bids for dispersal separately.
2. Schedule shipments to fit the needs of lenders, final venue, shipper, and organizer. Confirm the sched-

ule with all parties before finally booking it with the shipper.
3. Provide address labels for the crates.

7-2 RECEIPTS AND BILLS

When the returns have started on their way, issue a receipt to each lender. Calculate the prorated shipping expenses and issue invoices to exhibitors for any unpaid shipping/courier costs. If you chose to have an estimated shipping charge paid in advance and actual costs turned out to be less, reconcile the difference by issuing a refund to exhibitors. Check to be sure all invoices and participation fees have been paid and that everything is in order from the point of view of the business office.

7-3 RECORDS AND FILES

These final steps are vulnerable to being lost in the crush of other demands on the registrar's or exhibition coordinator's time. However, to maintain a professional and responsible operation, it is necessary to be sure they are not overlooked.

1. Cull files for essentials, discarding duplicates and making copies of appropriate documents for other departments to ensure that all necessary communication and accountability takes place. For example, copies or summaries of invoices should be provided to the development office for their final report on use of funds in a grant-supported project.
2. Enter data in the files of permanent collection objects and update computer records. Keeping track of an object's inclusion in exhibitions and publications ensures accurate object history and complete information for future scholarship. Labels on the back of each work showing the title, venues, and dates of the exhibition are part of this process, and if such labels were not placed on the reverse of works as they were received at the start of the exhibition, they can be placed there during final condition checks. Computer records should be updated, including location, condition, exhibition history, and publication information.

Once these tasks have been completed, the organizing registrar can relax—until requests for budget estimates for the next project come along.

CHAPTER 8

Traveling Exhibition Theory in Practice

8-1 MICHAEL SHERRILL RETROSPECTIVE

by Katherine Steiner
chief registrar, The Mint Museum

Michael tugs gently at a wall-mounted ceramic and metal sculpture of a leafy branch and it begins to vibrate, as if a sudden wind has risen in the gallery. The leaves make a light tinkling noise, but I say nothing, because he both made the piece and owns it, though I cringe a little, knowing that this piece and lots of its fragile friends are about to hit the road.

Though many would call Michael Sherrill a ceramist, he would not really identify himself in such a limiting way. He began his career with vessels and teapots, which became increasingly less functional, then moved into free-standing ceramic and metal botanical sculptures. His more recent work includes large, wall-mounted botanical sculptures and metal cylindrical structures. *Michael Sherrill Retrospective* featured a varied body of complex work that was a challenge to travel.

Crate construction is difficult for irregular objects. Michael built crates for newer work. If you choose to have the maker of the object build the crate, make sure you have a clear understanding with the artist about the details. Artists are not always skilled crate builders, and as borrower, the museum will probably insure the pieces. You do not want to send objects out unsafely packed or have the awkward conversation explaining that the artist does not really know how to build a crate. Before you incur additional costs, make sure everyone understands the expectations. Artists and museums often have different goals. We did not understand, for example, that Michael would build a crate for each piece instead of multiple pieces, so his crating bill was higher than expected, and we almost needed an extra truck to ship everything. We had crates for local loans built elsewhere and fitted out at the museum. We needed to factor extra time into packing the exhibition so that the shipper had time to pack on site. When the shipper underestimated the

complexity of the job, we found ourselves spending more time packing than originally estimated. Though preexisting crates can save money, we found that some for this exhibition were not suitable for extended travel and replaced or enhanced them.

Communicating information about packing, handling, and installation can be complex. A courier traveled to each venue, but it is impossible to oversee every single aspect of an installation. Two heavy columnar pieces required a mechanical lift and extra labor to hoist. We photographed the installation carefully and shared as much information as we could with the venues in advance. In addition, we chose to complete condition reports on a tablet, using inexpensive PDF software so that we could consolidate condition information and packing and installation notes. We especially liked the ability to zoom in on problem areas when we were not sure whether damage had occurred. If you use tablets in this manner, make sure you send enough devices to keep condition reports moving while installers and unpackers use the tablets for reference. We also found that some individuals were not comfortable using the tablets, adding an extra educational component (and time) to the project. No matter how professional the team is at each venue, be sure to communicate all expectations for the installation: who has access to the gallery, start and finish times, construction and painting completion dates, whether the casework needs to be in place before the exhibition arrives, necessary supplies, and any other details that are critical to the courier's comfort level.

With almost every traveling exhibition, there are **extras**. For this exhibition, some mounts would not fit in crates with objects. We used templates to make installation of wall-mounted pieces easier. Gold-leafed teapots needed to be handled with cotton gloves rather than nitrile. We packed special pillows that we found useful in supporting objects. All of these things went into a utility box traveling with the show. It helps to make this box distinctive, so that it can be located easily.

Never underestimate the value of **building relationships**. One of the loans has a vivid green glass snake slithering around a metal branch. The snake is installed by gently threading part of the branch through the snake's body and attaching the other part of the branch to support it below. By building trust with the lender, we were able to act as courier for the piece rather than incurring the expense of a lender's courier. We all know what a challenge it can be to work with living artists. Because Michael's studio is only a few hours from the museum, we could send staff from all levels to meet him and see the work. Each team member had frank conversations with him about their particular interests: how we wanted the design to look, how to install individual pieces, and, ultimately, why we preferred not to have his help during installation. When an object was damaged in transit to the first venue, it was easy to pick up the phone to discuss the best way to repair the piece.

Finally, just **a few quick notes**:

- Of course, you will number the crates so you know what is in each one, but be sure to make a note if you skip a number. There is nothing worse than having a crate list that goes to sixty but only counting fifty-nine crates.

- We found tablets extremely useful for reporting conditions. We could take as many pictures as we needed and zoom in on details. Best of all, the large number of images made it easy to identify where each flaw could be found.

- Send templates when objects are difficult to install. If hardware is not on an axis, make sure to add a level line to your templates, especially if the object does not have a clear orientation.

- If memory and instructions fail, call someone who helped install the exhibition at a previous venue to clear up the details.

Ultimately, prepare for everything possible with traveling exhibitions, especially for the certainty that the plan will change.

Michael Sherrill Retrospective was organized by The Mint Museum, Charlotte, North Carolina (October 27, 2018–April 7, 2019) and shown at The Renwick Gallery, Washington, DC (June 28, 2019–January 5, 2020) and Arizona State University Art Museum, Tempe, Arizona (February 29, 2020–June 27, 2020).

The glass snake is threaded onto the upper metal branch. While one person holds the snake, a second branch piece is attached. The snake is then lowered into place.
Photograph by Brandon Scott.

Collection of the Museum of Glass, Tacoma.
Photograph by Brandon Scott.

Many objects in the exhibition were particularly difficult to handle and pack.
Photograph by Brandon Scott.

Documenting how an object is packed is helpful for unpacking.
Photograph by Brandon Scott.

This crate arrived with foam feet, so more durable wooden feet are being added.
Photograph by Brandon Scott.

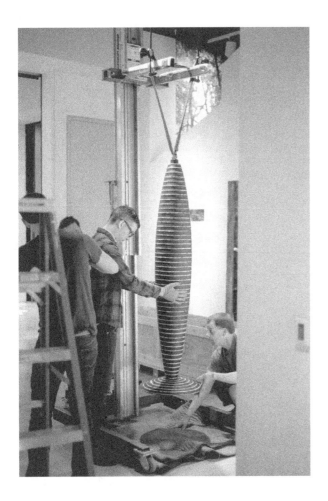

Describing how to lift a 300-pound column with a strap and a mechanical lift is much easier if you send images—better yet, a video.
Photograph by Brandon Scott.

Michael Sherrill Retrospective installed at the Mint Museum.
Photograph by Brandon Scott.

The Sampler Museum Exhibition Checklist

SAMPLE THE FUTURE EXHIBITION CHECKLIST

Exhibition Concept

The Sampler Museum presents *Sample the Future*, an exhibition of outstanding examples of samples. The exhibition includes three major types of objects: framed works (paintings, prints, photographs), textiles (quilts and costumes), and objects (jewelry, models, toys). The works are from the collection of The Sampler Museum and are borrowed from museums and private collections in various parts of the United States, Europe, and Japan. The show will appear first at The Sampler Museum, then travel to Sarasota and Maine, ending in Oslo.

Checklist

1 Pendant, *Future*, ca. 1912
  Tiffany and Company, Newark, New Jersey
  Diamond and silver, 1¾ × ½ in.
  Gift of Susan F. Middleton, 1934
  34.56 $56,000 The Sampler
             Museum

2 Edgar Westcott, American, 1856–1913
  Bear Mountain, 1898
  Oil on canvas, 16 × 28 in.
  Lent by the Holly Museum, gift of Daniel
   Sinclair, 1999
  1999.1.2 $500,000 Lebanon,
              CT

3 John Johansen, American, b. 1968
  Bear Mountain in Space, 2001
  Mixed media, 16 × 12 × 8 in.
  Purchase 2001 The Stanley Silver Fund
  2001.26.3 $40,000 The Sampler
             Museum

4 Advertising sign, *Sample the Future*, 2002
  Plywood and paint, 72 × 48 in.
  Lent by Emmitt $3,000 Dubuque, IA
   T. Small

5 Tom Talcott, American, b. 1946
  Taking the Country by Storm, 2002
  Oil on canvas, 36 × 24 in.
  Gift of Molly $25,000 The Sampler
   and Stanley   Museum
   Steele, 2002

6 Meredith Smith, American, b. 1937
  Countryside, 1987
  Quilt, cotton and polyester, 84 × 96 in.
  Lent by the artist $12,500 New York,
               NY

7 Meredith Smith, American, b. 1937
  Thoughts of Stars, 1993
  Quilt, cotton and polyester, 82½ × 90 in.
  Purchase 1996 $15,000 The Sampler
   Matilde Best   Museum
   Bequest Fund

8 Jonathan Small, American, b. 1955
  Out of Time, 1999
  Mixed media, 90 × 53 in.
  Lent by the $53,000 Bangor, ME
   Bangor
   Museum

9 Jonathan Small, American, b. 1955
  Taking the Lead, 1984
  Oil on canvas, 80 × 26 in.
  Lent by the New York Museum
  Gift of Mattie $85,000 New York,
   Melanek,   NY
   1992

10 Jonathan Small, American, b. 1955
  Smiling at the Night, 1988
  Stone, 42 × 63 × 20 in.
  Lent by the New York Museum
  Gift of Leslie $100,000 New York,
   and Harold   NY
   Small, 1990

11   Anonymous
      Tall Stories, 1967
      Oil on canvas, 24 × 30 in.
      Lent by the Museum of Greater Tampa
      Purchase $40,000   Tampa, FL
          1976, Greta
          Osbourne

12   Tempio Products, Tiffin, Ohio
      Space cars, ca. 1955
      Game with five pieces, box 20 × 15 × 4
      Lent by J. F. $450   Philadelphia,
          Kidder   PA

13   Fluid Product, Tokyo, Japan
      Space suit with helmet, ca. 1980
      Fabric, metal
      Suit 60 in. height, sleeves 19 in.
      Lent by Fluid $15,000   Tokyo, Japan
          Tokyo

14–25 Henry James Joyce
      Space futures, set of 12 prototype drawings
      Pencil and ink on paper, each 16 × 20 in.
          framed
      Lent by Los $100,000   Los Angeles,
          Angeles   total   CA
          Automobile
          Museum

26–28 Capodimonte Pottery, Naples, Italy
      Vases (three)
      Space forms with roses, 1989
      Each 25 in. tall, 8 in. diameter
      Lent by the $3,600   Naples, Italy
          Italian Arts   total
          Museum

29–40 Gander Monton, American, b. 1968
      Found in Space I-X11, 1998
      Computer-generated prints, each 22 × 28 in.
      Lent by the artist $12,000   Houston, TX
                           total

41   *Taurus 6*, 2000
      Space capsule model
      48 × 84 × 36 in.
      Lent by NASA $100,000   Houston, TX

42   Susan Finlay Silver
      Quiet Time, 2002
      Quilted cotton, 84 × 68 in.
      Lent by the artist $30,000   New York,
                                        NY

Generic RFP for Shipping

CHRISTOPHER SADE
formerly sales manager, Artex

Museum Service Representative
Museum Services Company
123 Museum Services Blvd.
Service Town, USA 12345

Dear Museum Services Representative,

We are in the process of putting together a budget for our exhibition *Sample the Future*, which opens in October. We would like to request estimates for consolidating, touring, and dispersal of the following loans.

Please note:

- All vehicles will be climate control (70° F ± 5°), dual drivers, air-ride (tractor and trailer suspension system), lift gate.
- The trucks must accommodate a courier on board, unless otherwise stated.
- The Western Museum of Art will be responsible for handling the insurance regarding this exhibition.

ITINERARY

October 20, 2020– January 10, 2021	The Western Museum of Art
February 10, 2021– May 13, 2021	The Mid-Western Museum of Art
June 12, 2021– September 11, 2021	The Northeastern Museum of Art
October 11, 2021– January 5, 2022	The European Museum of Art
February 8, 2022– May 10, 2022	The Southeastern Museum

Note: Overseas Freight Forwarding Services will handle the international portion of the tour. The shipment should be delivered to North East International Airport on or about June 1, 2021. The shipment will return to Southeast International Airport on or about January 22, 2022. All dates are subject to confirmation.

Crating

All two-dimensional (2-D) works of art should be crated according to our specifications. Please keep in mind that crating should be compliant with European Union (EU) standards. All works listed in numbers 1 to 5 that follow require on-site crating, and the packed works stay with the institution until collection is made during consolidation. Please include these pickups in your consolidation to our museum.

Dimensions are provided in inches, listing H × L × W.

1. ABC Museum of the Alphabetic Art, Eastern USA
   Museum Address
   City, State, Zip Code
   Contact and Phone number

   (6) 2-D works, oil on canvas, each 24 × 36 × 4 inches (framed)
   (2) 2-D works, oil on board, each 30 × 30 × 3 inches (framed)
   (1) Object, mixed media, 15 × 65 × 6 inches

2. Private Collector, Eastern USA
   Private Residence Address
   City, State, Zip Code
   Contact, Additional Contact and Phone number

   (2) 2-D works, charcoal on paper, each 48 × 48 × 6 inches (framed)
   (1) 2-D work, pencil on paper, 60 × 72 × 4 inches (framed)
   (1) 2-D work, ink on paper, 80 × 80 × 4 inches (framed)

3. Private Collector, Northeast USA
   Private Residence Address
   City, State, Zip Code
   Contact, Additional Contact, and Phone number

   (2) Bronze sculptures, each 24 × 12 × 24 inches
   (1) Marble bust, 30 × 20 × 22 inches

4. Contemporary Museum of America, Mid-Atlantic USA
Museum Address
City, State, Zip Code
Contact and Phone number

(1) Sculpture, 80 × 24 × 20 inches

5. 123 Numbers Institute of Counting, Southeast USA
Museum Address
City, Sate, Zip Code
Contact and Phone number

(8) 2-D works, oil on canvas, each 16 × 18 × 2 inches (framed)

6. The Museum of Art, Northeast USA
Museum Address
City, State, Zip Code
Contact and Phone number

3 crates measuring:
55 × 35 × 35 inches
25 × 20 × 36 inches
12 × 12 × 18 inches

7. The Art Museum of America, Mid-Atlantic USA
Museum Address
City, State, Zip Code
Contact and Phone number

1 crate measuring:
100 × 80 × 18 inches

8. Historical Society of America, Midwest USA
Museum Address
City, State, Zip Code
Contact and Phone number

2 crates measuring:
55 × 35 × 33 inches
25 × 30 × 36 inches

9. The Museum of Objects, Mid-Atlantic USA
Museum Address
City, State, Zip Code
Contact and Phone number

3 crates measuring:
65 × 30 × 55 inches
55 × 50 × 36 inches
22 × 22 × 18 inches

10. Museum of Paintings, Southwest USA
Museum Address
City, State, Zip Code
Contact and Phone number

1 crate measuring:
110 × 120 × 12 inches

Consolidation
[Note to reader: Include pick-up address; city, state, zip code; contact and phone number; and facility information, that is, hours of operation, truck accessibility, labor situation, etc.]

Instructions: Exclusive-use, climate controlled, dual-driver service is required. Multiple stops are acceptable for consolidation stops 1, 2, and 3 (courier is not required). Stops number 4 and 5 require separate, exclusive trucks, and a courier will ride on board to meet loan requirements. Please quote the most efficient method of collection for lenders 6 through 10.

Dispersal Information
Please pick up from the Southeastern Museum and return loans to the original lenders, unless otherwise specified.

Recap of Our Request

1. Crating cost as outlined above. European venue requires crating to meet EU compliance.
2. Consolidation cost as outlined above. All loans will consolidate to the Western Museum of Art.
3. Tour cost as outlined in our itinerary.
4. Dispersal cost will begin from the Southeastern Museum, and all loans should return to the original lender, unless otherwise specified
5. Grand total regarding cost of services.

Reminder: Exclusive-use transportation is required unless otherwise specified. We ask for the van to be climate controlled (maintaining a temperature of 70° F) and air-ride equipped and to have a lift gate with the capacity to handle our shipment requirements. In addition, transportation requires dual-driver service.

Please let me know if you have questions regarding this request for proposal. I look forward to your response.

Sincerely,

Museum Registrar/Collections Manager
The Western Museum of Art

Sample Traveling Exhibition Contract

[Please note: This contract is presented as a sample only. Consult legal counsel before adopting or using this form.]

GENERAL INFORMATION
Exhibition title:
Organizing exhibitor:
Address:
Contact name:
Contact title:
Telephone:
Mobile:
E-mail:

Loan period dates:
Exhibition public opening date:
Exhibition first event:
Exhibition closing date:

Participation fee:
Fee includes:
   <<use of the objects to be exhibited (see Appendix A), labels (electronic copy), text panels, all costs for Organizer's courier at installation and deinstallation, crates, care and handling guidelines, condition report books, materials for design and programming, wall-to-wall insurance for the exhibition, and a limited number of catalogues>>
Other requirements:
Insurance:
Insurance value:
Credit:

1. AGREEMENT TO BORROW

This Agreement is made this <<date>> between <<Legal name and location of organizer>> (<<Short name for organizer>> or "Organizer"), and <<Legal name and location of exhibitor>> ("the Exhibitor").

The Organizer has prepared an exhibition for circulation titled <<Title of Exhibition>> ("the Exhibition"). The Exhibitor desires to display the Exhibition according to the terms and conditions set forth herein.

The Exhibitor hereby agrees to borrow and the Organizer agrees to lend the Exhibition for the purpose of exhibition ("loan purpose") on the Exhibitor's premises (the "approved location") during the period of <<dates>> (the "exhibition period"); <<amount of time>> will be allowed before and after the exhibition period for transportation, unpacking/packing, and installation/deinstallation. The Exhibitor agrees to pay in consideration of this loan the amount of $ <<participation fee>>.

The Exhibition consists of the objects set forth in Appendix A (which is attached hereto and made part of this agreement), object mounts and/or installation hardware, text and other panels and labels (collectively, the "exhibition materials").

The Exhibitor will comply with all special instructions of the Organizer as outlined herein and in all written registration notes accompanying the Exhibition with respect to condition, care, handling, installation, presentation, security, and packing of the Exhibition. Care and handling instructions can be found in Appendix B, attached.

2. FEES/PAYMENT SCHEDULE

The Exhibitor agrees to pay the loan fee to the Organizer in two installments as follows: (1) $_____ to be sent with the executed original of the Agreement and (2) $_____ to be paid by the first day of the exhibition period, or not later than <<date>>. The Organizer will provide an invoice to the Exhibitor for all payments.

The fee for the Exhibition includes use of a fully researched and assembled exhibition with labels, educational materials, publicity packet, and insurance. It also includes catalogs and/or brochures, as noted below. Packing and crating are included. All costs for the Organizer's courier(s), who will help with installation and deinstallation, are included. If lenders require couriers for specific works, the cost of those couriers (transport, lodging, and per diem) will be borne by the Exhibitor. Shipping costs are not included in the exhibition fee.

The Exhibitor is responsible for all local costs incurred in presenting the Exhibition, including but not limited to its unpacking/repacking, crate storage, installation, publicity, programming, receptions, and so forth. The Exhibitor also is responsible for any additional costs that may be specifically outlined in correspondence between the Organizer and the Exhibitor.

3. INSURANCE

The Organizer, as part of the exhibition loan fee, shall continuously insure the exhibition materials on a wall-to-wall basis against all risks of physical loss or damage from any external cause except wear and tear, gradual deterioration, terrorism, and other exclusions standard to fine arts policies. The Exhibitor shall report to the Registrar, <<name of organizer>>, any damage to the exhibition materials while in transit to or while on the Exhibitor's premises, regardless of who may be responsible.

Report to: <<name>>, Registrar; phone: <<number>>

The Exhibitor must preserve all parts, packing materials, and other evidence or result of damage and provide photographs documenting damage and action taken in response. The Exhibitor shall be held responsible for any damage to the exhibition materials that results from its negligence or failure to comply with this agreement, including, but not limited to, its failure to comply with the Organizer's registration notes and instructions regarding security, unpacking/repacking, handling, installation/deinstallation, and shipment, as well as any and all damages to the exhibition materials during the loan period that the Organizer does not recover from an insurance carrier.

4. EXHIBITION DISPLAY/RESTRICTIONS

The Exhibitor shall exhibit all exhibition materials as listed in Appendix A, unless express written permission to the contrary has been obtained in advance from the Organizer. The Exhibitor will not show the Exhibition at more than one location without prior written permission from the Organizer. Further, the Exhibitor agrees to provide a secure and environmentally suitable storage area for any exhibition materials withdrawn from the Exhibition (as outlined in the care and handling regulations, Appendix B) for any reason and/or to pay any additional transportation or courier costs that may be incurred as a result of withdrawals of exhibition materials from the Exhibition.

The Organizer shall provide the Exhibitor with a detailed set of guidelines for the handling and display of the exhibition materials <<amount of time>> before the opening of the exhibition. The Exhibitor shall make such guidelines accessible to its installation and design staff, and other applicable staff, and shall be responsible for ensuring strict adherence to such guidelines.

5. CREDIT LINES/SPONSORSHIPS

The following credit shall be included on invitations and official press releases and posted at the entrance to the exhibition:

<<Exhibition title>> was organized by the <<name of organizer>>. The exhibition has received funding from <<Funders names>>. Additional support has been received from <<name(s) of foundations, corporations, and individuals>>.

Other promotional and related programmatic materials will carry the first sentence of the above credit.

6. SHIPPING

The Exhibitor is responsible for the cost of shipping, which will be prorated [or actual, or a combination of the two] among all exhibitors. The estimated cost of shipping is $____ and is payable upon receipt of the exhibition materials. Adjustments to shipping payments will be made at the end of the tour of the Exhibition.

For foreign venues, and for Alaskan and Hawaiian venues, the Exhibitor must pay round-trip shipping costs from the port-of-exit in the contiguous forty-eight states of the United States in addition to the prorated shipping costs. The foreign exhibitor also is required to pay all charges for customs clearance upon the Exhibition's leaving and reentering the United States.

The Organizer, or the previous Exhibitor, shall pack the exhibition materials for shipment to the Exhibitor and arrange for their delivery to the Exhibitor not later than the first day of the loan period, by a carrier selected and scheduled in advance by the Organizer. The Exhibitor agrees to meet all transportation schedules required for the safety of objects and the timely shipment to other exhibitors. The Exhibitor agrees that if it is unable to receive and ship the Exhibition in compliance with the necessary transportation schedule, it will absorb the cost of an acceptable interim storage facility and other expenses resulting from its inability to comply with such schedule.

7. PACKING/HANDLING/CARE/CONDITION REPORTING

The Exhibitor shall ensure that all packing and unpacking instructions given by the Organizer are followed explicitly by competent packers, not volunteers or interns, who are trained in museum object handling and that the exhibition materials are handled with special care at all times to protect against damage or deterioration. All unloading, unpacking, handling, repacking, and reloading shall occur under the surveillance of the Exhibitor's registrar in consultation with the Exhibitor's conservators and security staff, or applicable staff. Exhibition material shall be handled with at least the same care as the Exhibitor uses in handling its own property of a similar nature.

In preparing exhibition materials for their outgoing shipment, the Exhibitor shall ensure that the exhibition materials are packed in the same manner in which they were delivered to the Exhibitor and are thus prepared for outgoing shipment no later than the last day of the loan period. The Exhibitor shall notify immediately, by telephone or email, the Registrar, <<name of organizer>>, of any loss or damage to the packing materials or packing crates that might impair their ability to protect the exhibition materials. The Exhibitor, at its own expense, shall, in consultation with the Registrar, <<name of organizer>>, replace with comparable materials packing materials or crates lost or damaged while in its care.

The Exhibitor must examine the exhibition materials after a 24-hour acclimation period and within seven days of their receipt, and report on their condition. Each object will be accompanied by an illustrated condition report, which will be annotated as appropriate and signed by the Exhibitor's conservator or registrar and by an authorized representative of the Organizer and/or lender representative present at unpacking, installation, deinstallation, and repacking on the Exhibitor's premises. The Exhibitor will ensure that the condition reports travel with the objects to the next Exhibition site; that the condition of the Objects is checked regularly while in Exhibitor's possession; and that any significant change in an Object's condition while in the possession of the Exhibitor is noted on the report. Any damage to the objects discovered during the initial condition check or at any time during the loan period must be reported immediately in writing, with photographic documentation, to the Registrar, <<name of organizer>>. The Exhibitor agrees that it may not alter or repair any of the exhibition materials without first obtaining the express written permission of the Organizer.

8. FACILITIES
The Exhibitor shall, at its own expense, provide adequate security and environmental conditions for the exhibition materials, and shall comply with any and all special instructions put forth by the Organizer for the care of the exhibition materials. The Exhibitor shall provide the Organizer with a copy of its General Facility Report (GFR), which is available from the American Alliance of Museums; the Organizer will review the GFR as part of the contractual process.

All objects must be displayed according to guidelines provided by the Organizer.

The Exhibitor shall assign security guard(s), as noted, to the exhibition space during open hours. As a security minimum during closed hours, the Exhibitor must have electronic surveillance systems that report to a central station that is manned 24 hours per day. Permission to use plants in the galleries must be obtained from the Registrar, <<name of organizer>>; food and drink will NOT be allowed in the exhibition galleries, storage areas, or anywhere the exhibition materials are kept.

The Exhibitor shall maintain 50% ± 5% relative humidity and temperature of 68°–72° F. Light levels shall be maintained according to the guidelines provided.

The public shall be admitted to the exhibition without discrimination or segregation, and regardless of race, color, creed, sex, age, or national origin. In addition, the Exhibitor represents that there is full access to the exhibition for the physically disabled, as stipulated in Section 504 of Federal Public Law 93-112, as amended. The Exhibitor shall be in compliance with the Americans with Disabilities Act (Public Law 101-336, enacted July 26, 1990).

9. PUBLICITY
The Organizer will supply the Exhibitor with a press release and a selection of photographs that may be used in preparing publicity and related materials for the Exhibition. The Exhibitor agrees to clear its own press release, Exhibition advertisements, and Exhibition information posted on the Exhibitor's website with the Public Relations department of the Organizer before use or distribution.

The Exhibitor shall forward promptly to <<name of contact person>>, <<name of organizer>>, copies of all publicity releases, reviews, published articles, and other similar matter relating to the exhibition. At the end of the loan period, the Exhibitor will forward attendance figures to the Organizer.

The Organizer reserves to itself the right to copy, photograph, or reproduce the exhibition materials. The Exhibitor shall not permit any of the exhibition materials to be copied, photographed, or reproduced and, in the event of their public exhibition, shall contain in their photography guidelines a statement advising persons attending the Exhibition that the exhibition materials may not be copied, photographed, or reproduced. Notwithstanding the foregoing sentence, the Exhibitor may cause the exhibition materials to be photographed for curatorial and registrarial purposes, provided that such photographs are made without removal of frames or mounts and are not released without the Organizer's prior written consent and provided further that the Organizer will be supplied with duplicate of the images.

The Organizer will provide the Exhibitor with <<number>> copies of the catalog <<*Title*>>. Additional copies of the catalog can be purchased at cost from the <<name of organizer>>'s shop.

10. DAMAGES, BREACH OF AGREEMENT

The Exhibitor must notify the Organizer in writing to cancel the signed Agreement. The parties understand that it will be difficult, if not impossible, to calculate or estimate the serious and substantial damage to the Organizer that would be caused by breach of this Agreement by the Exhibitor, and therefore, the parties agree that in the event the Exhibitor cancels this Agreement prior to the beginning of the loan period, for any reason whatsoever (other than the inability of the Organizer to perform hereunder), the Exhibitor shall pay to the Organizer, as liquidated damages and not as a penalty, the total loan fee, which the balance shall be due and payable immediately upon such cancellation. However, in the event that the Organizer arranges for an alternate venue for the Exhibition acceptable to the Organizer during the loan period, the fees received from that venue, less the cost of procuring such alternate venue, shall be applied to reduce the amount payable to the Organizer under this paragraph. The Organizer, however, shall have no obligation to procure such alternate sponsor and the Exhibitor is entitled to no reduction of the loan fee for the Organizer's failure to procure such alternate venue.

In the event the Exhibitor fails to pay any amount when due under this Agreement, including but not limited to costs payable under paragraphs 1 and 2 above, such failure continuing for a period of 10 business days, the amount at the rate of 15% per annum from the date the unpaid amount originally was due will accrue until the late payment is received by the Organizer. Nothing in this Agreement shall be construed as an express or implied agreement by the Organizer to forbear in the collection of any delin-

quent payment. Further, this Agreement shall not be construed as in any way giving the Exhibitor the right, express or implied, to fail to make timely payments hereunder, whether upon payment of such interest rate or otherwise. Should the Exhibitor not receive the first payment before the scheduled shipment date, the Organizer reserves the right to cancel the contract at its own discretion.

The parties further understand that, although the Organizer shall endeavor to make all reasonable effort to assure delivery of the Exhibition to the Exhibitor prior to the scheduled opening as stated above:

a) In the event that the Organizer is unable to perform hereunder, the Organizer shall promptly refund to the Exhibitor the fee already paid by the Exhibitor in full and complete satisfaction of its obligation to the Exhibitor. Upon prior written notice, the Organizer may terminate this Agreement prior to the beginning of the loan period for events beyond its control. The Exhibitor shall release, indemnify, and hold the Organizer harmless from and against any and all loss arising from the Exhibitor's inability to display the Exhibition because of loss or damage to the exhibition materials while in transit; and

b) In the event the Organizer for any reason withdraws any work of art from the Exhibition while it is in circulation, the Exhibitor shall promptly comply with all packing and shipping instructions given by the Organizer in the course of such withdrawal. The Organizer shall concurrently reimburse the Exhibitor for its costs and expenses of packing and shipping incurred by such withdrawal.

11. NOTICES

Except as otherwise required specifically herein, all notices and other communication provided for or permitted hereunder shall be made by hand-delivery, prepaid, first-class mail, fax, or e-mail. All notices are considered delivered when delivered by hand, four days after deposit of first-class mail, and when receipt is acknowledged for fax and e-mail. In the case of extreme emergencies, immediate verbal consent should be sought by the Exhibitor and followed as soon as possible in writing.

If to the Organizer
Name and title
Address
Phone

Mobile
E-mail

If to the Exhibitor
Name and title
Address
Phone
Mobile
E-mail

12. SUCCESSORS AND ASSIGNS
The Agreement shall inure to the benefit of and be binding on the successors of each of the parties. This Agreement may not be assigned by either party without the prior written consent of the other.

13. WAIVERS, REMEDIES
No delay on the part of any party hereto in exercising any right, power, or privilege hereunder shall operate as a waiver thereof, nor shall any waiver on the part of any party hereto of any right, power, or privilege hereunder operate as a waiver of any right, power, or privilege hereunder.

14. ENTIRE AGREEMENT
This Agreement, together with all written special instructions accompanying the Exhibition, is intended by the parties as a final expression of their agreement and is a complete and exclusive statement of the agreement and understanding of the parties. This Agreement supersedes all prior agreements and understandings between the parties with respect to the subject matter contained herein.

15. ATTORNEYS' FEES
In any action or proceeding brought to enforce any provision of this Agreement, or where any provision hereof is validly asserted as a defense, the successful party shall be entitled to recover reasonable attorneys' fees in addition to any other available remedy.

16. SEVERABILITY
In the event that any one or more of the provisions contained herein, or the application thereof in any circumstances, is held invalid, illegal, or unenforceable in any respect for any reason, the validity, legality, and enforceability of any such provision in every other respect and of the remaining provisions hereof shall not in any way be impaired or affected, it being intended that all of the rights and privileges contained herein shall be enforceable to the fullest extent permitted by law.

17. GOVERNING LAW
This Agreement shall be governed by and construed in accordance with the State of <<organizer's location>>.

SIGNATURES

18. APPENDIXES/ATTACHMENTS/SCHEDULES

This contract was drawn up initially by the Office of General Counsel, University of Pennsylvania, for the University of Pennsylvania Museum of Archaeology and Anthropology. It was modified at The Newark Museum, expanded with Smithsonian Institution Traveling Exhibition Service (SITES) statements, and edited by two lawyers.

Model Traveling Exhibition Contract

[Please note: This contract is provided as a model only. Consult legal counsel before adopting or using this form.]

EXHIBITION AGREEMENT

[For an exhibition organized by one institution and lent to one or more institutions by the organizing institution for a fee]

This Exhibition Agreement (the "Agreement") is made by and between [Name and address of the Organizing institution] (the "Organizer") and [Name and address of the Exhibiting institution] (the "Exhibitor").

The Organizer has assembled an exhibition titled [Name of Exhibition] (the "Exhibition"). The Exhibitor agrees to display the Exhibition in accordance with the following terms and conditions:

I. The Exhibition

The Exhibition consists of those works of art (a "Work" or "Works") listed in Attachment I (the "Checklist"). The Organizer reserves the right to withdraw a Work or Works from the Exhibition at any time for any reason. The Exhibitor agrees that it will show the Exhibition in its entirety, without deletions or additions, unless specific written permission for any such change is obtained from the Organizer before the Exhibition opens at the Exhibitor's location. The Exhibitor may not change the title of the Exhibition without the Organizer's advance written approval.

II. Exhibition Schedule

    Locations   Dates

Any proposed change in an Exhibition location or date of showing must be approved by the Organizer in writing at least 90 days before the Exhibition opens at that location.

III. Financial Arrangements

A. The Exhibitor agrees to pay a participation fee of [_____] Dollars ($[____]) to the Organizer, of which one-half, [_____] Dollars ($[____]), is payable upon signing this Agreement, and the balance is payable on the opening of the Exhibition at the Exhibitor's location. The Organizer will invoice the Exhibitor for each payment. Payment shall be made to [Name of Organizing Institution] by check or other means agreed upon by the Organizer and the Exhibitor within 30 days of receipt of such invoice. The Exhibitor also agrees to pay its share of prorated transportation costs, not to exceed $[____]. Transportation costs will include Organizer's courier expenses (travel and per diem for [__] couriers for [__] days). Prorated costs will be based on actual expenses and will be invoiced as soon as they are available.

B. The Exhibitor will bear all local costs incurred in presenting the Exhibition, including, but not limited to, on-site insurance coverage of the Works; promotion, publicity, previews, unpacking and repacking the Works on the Exhibitor's premises, installation costs, storage on the Exhibitor's premises (if necessary), educational programs, entertainment, and receptions.

C. The Exhibitor may seek sponsorship funding to cover its costs for showing the Exhibition, including all local costs and the Exhibitor's participation fee (collectively, the "Local Costs"). To avoid sponsorship conflicts, if the Exhibitor seeks sponsorship funding for its Local Costs, it agrees to consult with the Organizer and obtain the Organizer's prior written consent to such sponsors. The Organizer agrees not to unreasonably withhold or delay its consent.

IV. Credits and Acknowledgments

A. The following credit line will be displayed prominently at the entrance to the galleries where the

Exhibition is installed and shall also appear on all printed materials related to the Exhibition including, but not limited to, press releases, invitations, announcements, brochures, posters, advertising, or other publicity:

Organized by [Name of Organizing Institution].
Sponsored by [Name of Sponsor].

The Exhibitor will encourage all news media to include this credit line in reporting on the Exhibition.

B. Should sponsorship of the Exhibitor's Local Costs be secured, the Exhibitor and the Organizer will mutually agree upon an appropriate credit line. Such acknowledgment shall appear in a separate credit line below the Organizer's credit line in a typeface compatible with and no larger than that used in the Organizer's credit line.

C. If the Organizer secures additional financial support for the Exhibition, it reserves the right to change the credit line and the Exhibitor agrees to use such revised credit line. Any revisions to the credit line(s) will be communicated to the Exhibitor in writing. Such revisions shall be included in all print and promotional matter not already in production or existence at the time the Exhibitor receives such revision.

V. Packing and Shipping

A. The Organizer's Registrar will make all arrangements for shipping of the Exhibition to and from the Exhibitor. The Organizer's courier will accompany the Exhibition during its travel, and the courier's expenses will be included in the transportation costs. The Registrars of the Organizer and the Exhibitor will determine mutually convenient dates for the inbound and outbound shipment of the Exhibition within the limits imposed by the Exhibition Schedule set forth above.

B. The Exhibitor agrees to accept delivery of the Exhibition directly into a secure, climate-controlled area on its premises, where the Organizer's courier will inspect the delivered Exhibition materials. The Exhibitor will provide competent packers for unpacking and repacking the Exhibition. Unpacking will not take place until 24 hours after delivery. The Exhibitor agrees to store crates and packing materials for the Exhibition in climate controlled areas meeting the temperature and humidity standards set forth in Section VIII, below.

C. The Exhibitor agrees to deinstall and have the Exhibition packed and ready for shipping after the Exhibition closes, according to the mutually agreed-upon schedule. Deinstallation and repacking will take place promptly after the Exhibition closes, under the supervision of the Organizer's courier. All the Works must be repacked in their original wrapping materials. No changes in packing systems or materials may be made without the prior written approval of the Organizer.

D. If, under any circumstances, the Exhibitor cannot receive the Exhibition on the scheduled date or cannot prepare the Exhibition for its scheduled reshipment in a timely manner, the Exhibitor will advise the Organizer's Registrar immediately. The Exhibitor agrees to reimburse the Organizer for any additional costs incurred by the Organizer due to the Exhibitor's inability to receive the Exhibition or to ship the Exhibition from its premises in a timely manner.

VI. Condition Reports and Procedures in the Event of Loss or Damage

A. The Organizer will provide an initial condition report and photograph for each Work in the Exhibition, contained in a condition report notebook that will travel with the Exhibition. These condition reports are to be annotated as appropriate and will be signed and dated by the Organizer's courier and an authorized member of the Exhibitor's staff at the time of unpacking and immediately prior to repacking.

B. While on the Exhibitor's premises, the Works will be checked regularly by a qualified member of the Exhibitor's staff. Any change in condition of a Work will be noted on its condition report and reported immediately to the Organizer in the manner set forth below. If any Work is discovered to be in unstable or otherwise vulnerable physical condition, the Exhibitor will withdraw such Work from the Exhibition immediately.

C. No Work will be removed from its frame or other permanent mounting, and the Exhibitor will not make or permit the making of any repairs or perform any remedial action on any Work, without prior written authorization from the Organizer, except in case of an emergency (i) at the direction of an authorized Organizer's staff member on the Exhibitor's premises, or (ii) for procedures needed to prevent threatened damage or to arrest further damage in case of an accident, water leak, fire, flood, earthquake, or other immediate threat in circumstances where there is not sufficient time to allow contact to be made with the Organizer's staff.

D. If (i) any Work is damaged, lost, stolen, or subject to emergency procedures, (ii) there is any change in the condition of any Work, or (iii) a withdrawal of any Work becomes necessary, the Exhibitor will, in each such instance, immediately report such event and its cause, if known, to any Organizer staff member on the Exhibitor's premises or, if no Organizer staff member is present, to the Organizer's Registrar by telephone at [phone number]. If the Organizer's Registrar cannot be reached immediately, the Exhibitor will then notify the Organizer's security station at [phone number]. In any such event, the Exhibitor will comply with the instructions of authorized Organizer staff with respect to the affected Work.

E. Any damage to or change in the condition of any Work will be photographed by the Exhibitor immediately at the time of discovery and the photograph(s) will be included in a written report describing the following: the event and its cause, if known; the damage or deterioration, if any; the steps taken by the Exhibitor; the condition of the Work; and the Exhibitor's recommendations. A copy of such report will be sent by fax to the attention of the Organizer's Registrar at [phone number] and a hard copy sent by overnight courier to the Organizer's Registrar. The Exhibitor will provide promptly any additional information concerning such event that the Organizer may reasonably request.

F. In situations requiring immediate action, authorized Organizer staff may provide verbal consent and direction concerning any necessary treatment or handling of a Work, to be confirmed in writing. After permission is given by the Organizer, the Exhibitor shall require the person treating the affected Work to document fully any treatment and to append the documentation to the condition report notebook together with a copy of the Organizer's written permission for such treatment.

VII. Installation

A. The Exhibition must be installed in accordance with the Organizer's specifications, which will be provided to the Exhibitor at least [___] months prior to its receipt of the Exhibition.

B. The Works must be exhibited in the frames supplied and will be provided with hanging devices that may not be removed or repositioned. The Exhibitor may not affix other types of hanging devices to the Works, without written authorization from the Organizer.

C. The Exhibitor will be responsible for and bear all expenses of the installation of the Exhibition, including, but not limited to, the following: construction, exhibition furnishings and furniture, lighting, and graphics. Installation of the Works will not take place until all construction and painting activities in the Exhibition galleries have been completed. The Organizer will provide a checklist and other manuscript materials on computer disk, which will be used by the Exhibitor to produce its own object and introductory/ explanatory text labels in its preferred format. The content of the Exhibition texts, however, may not be altered or revised by the Exhibitor without the written permission of the Organizer.

VIII. Environment

A. The Exhibitor will ensure that proper standards of environmental control are maintained in spaces where the Works and their packing materials are stored or displayed, with particular attention given to maintaining acceptable light and humidity levels. No Work will be permitted to come into direct contact with any light fixtures or any heating, air conditioning, ventilation, or electrical outlets.

B. Relative humidity levels will be maintained in the range of [__]% to [__]%. There must not be more than a [_]% fluctuation in relative humidity during a 24-hour period.

C. A stable temperature will be maintained between [__]°F and [__]°F.

D. The Exhibitor will not allow any Works to be exposed to sunlight or fluorescent lights (unless the fluorescent fixtures have been fitted with ultraviolet filters) or excessive light levels. The required light level for [type of object] is [_] foot-candles ([__] lux).

IX. Security and Safety

The Exhibitor will be responsible for the security and safety of the Works while they are on its premises from the time of delivery until they leave for their next destination. The Organizer will arrange for the security of the Works during transit, and the Exhibitor agrees to cooperate with the Organizer for this purpose. The Exhibitor also agrees to confer with the Organizer concerning security matters relating to the Exhibition while on its premises and to provide authorized Organizer staff with such information about the Exhibitor's security as they may reasonably request. The minimum security to be provided by the Exhibitor is set forth in Attachment II, but the Exhibitor agrees that in no event shall the security protection provided for the Exhibition be less than what it provides for works of similar value and condition in its own collections.

X. Insurance and Risk of Loss

A. Insurance coverage for the Exhibition in transit will be provided by the Organizer, under its own Fine Arts Insurance Policy. The Organizer will provide the Exhibitor, prior to the delivery of the Exhibition to the Exhibitor, with a Certificate of Insurance naming the Exhibitor as an Additional Insured under such coverage.

B. The Exhibitor will provide wall-to-wall on-site insurance coverage for the Exhibition while at the Exhibitor's premises and will provide the Organizer with a Certificate of Insurance naming the Organizer an Additional Insured under such coverage. Such coverage shall be in such amounts and subject to such conditions as are reasonably satisfactory to the Organizer.

C. The Exhibitor agrees to follow the Organizer's reasonable instructions, including those given by authorized Organizer staff at the site of the Exhibition, regarding matters of safety and security for the Works and their handling, packing, unpacking, conditioning, installation, and shipping for the Exhibition.

XI. Photography, Reproductions, and Publicity

A. As outlined in Attachment III, the Organizer shall provide the Exhibitor with a suggested press release and selected photographs, slides, and color transparencies of Works from the Exhibition specifically for use in promotional articles, pamphlets, entrance tickets, advertising, the Exhibitor's website, and other similar promotional and educational material relating to the Exhibition, as well as for television programs reviewing or discussing the Exhibition. Except with the written consent of the Organizer, only reproductions and photographs of objects provided and/or duplicated from those provided by the Organizer may be used in connection with the Exhibitor's showing of the Exhibition. The Exhibitor agrees that all press releases, invitations, announcements, electronic media, and other promotional matter produced by the Exhibitor concerning the Exhibition will carry the full title of the Exhibition as set forth on page 1 of this Agreement and the Organizer's credit line referred to in Section IV above.

B. Except as provided in this Agreement, the Exhibitor will not allow photographs of any Works in the Exhibition to be taken for any reason without the prior written consent of the Organizer, or any other reproductions of any type in any medium to be made, except for photographs (i) required in accordance with Section VI above, (ii) at installation for archival or documentary purposes outlined in Section VII above, or (iii) as otherwise authorized in advance in writing by the Organizer. Exhibitor will prohibit photography by the public and will post an appropriate notice of the prohibition in the Exhibition area.

C. Photography, filming, and videography of the Exhibition, including television coverage, may be permitted for documentary, educational, or publicity purposes related to the Exhibition, but only if supervised by a member of the Exhibitor's professional staff.

D. All authorized photography is subject to the following restrictions:

1. Framed Works may not be removed from their frames.
2. Lights must be at least [__] feet away from any Work.
3. Total wattage of all lights will not exceed [___] watts.
4. Photography may be done only on the premises of the Exhibitor, under the supervision of an appropriate member of the Exhibitor's staff.
5. The Works will at all times be protected from contact with photographic and video equipment, and such equipment will not be permitted to be hazardously close to any Work.

E. Copyrights of third parties may apply to photographic materials provided for promotional and educational reproduction. The Organizer assumes full responsibility for negotiating permissions on behalf of itself and the Exhibitor, and for paying any applicable fees or royalties for reproduction of images relative to copyrights that may be held by or on behalf of artists or artists' estates. The Organizer assumes no responsibility for any fees or royalties claimed by artists or on their behalf with regard to any unauthorized reproduction, whether by photograph, film, or other medium, of the Works in the Exhibition made or occurring during the showing of the Exhibition by the Exhibitor. Compliance with copyright laws and observance of the reproduction rights of any third party occurring during the showing of the Exhibition by the Exhibitor shall be the responsibility of the Exhibitor, which agrees to indemnify, hold harmless, and defend the Organizer from and against all liabilities, losses, or expenses arising out of any claim by a third party of a violation of copyright laws or reproduction rights occurring during the showing of the Exhibition by the Exhibitor and any unauthorized use by the Exhibitor of a reproduction of a Work in the Exhibition.

F. To the extent not retained by third parties, the copyright for all reproductions of Works in the Exhibition is retained by the Organizer.

G. The Exhibitor agrees to send the Organizer drafts or copies of all proposed publicity materials for approval, such approval not to be unreasonably withheld. The Exhibitor will remit copies of any printed or electronic publicity or educational material relating to the Exhibition, together with a complete publicity report as specified in Attachment III, to the Organizer no later than 60 days after the Exhibition closes at the Exhibitor's location.

XII. Catalogs and Sales Materials

A. Copies of the catalog published by the Organizer may be ordered, subject to availability, at the wholesale price of $[__] (suggested retail price is $[__]) each, plus shipping and handling. The Exhibitor will notify the Organizer of the number of catalogs it wishes to order by [date].

B. Arrangements, if any, with respect to reproductions of, or other products relating to, the Works will be the subject of a separate agreement.

XIII. Right of Cancellation; Force Majeure

A. In the event that, less than [___] months before the scheduled opening of the Exhibition at the Exhibitor's location, the Exhibitor must cancel the Exhibition for any reason, except its untimely arrival at the Exhibitor's premises, the Exhibitor agrees to pay the unpaid balance of the participation fee. If the Exhibitor finds an alternative institution, agreeable to the Organizer, to show the Exhibition during the same time period, or at another time reasonably acceptable to the Organizer, the Exhibitor shall then only be liable to the Organizer for such part of the Exhibition fee not paid by such alternative institution and any additional transportation costs.

B. In no event will the Organizer be held responsible, nor will the Exhibitor be relieved of its responsibility to pay the participation fee, if inclement weather, earthquakes, accident, riot, strikes, or other similar acts over which the Organizer has no control, prevent the delivery of the Exhibition or portions of the Exhibition as scheduled.

XIV. Disputes; Limitation of Liability and Indemnification

A. Both the Organizer and the Exhibitor agree to use their best efforts to resolve through discussion and negotiation to their mutual satisfaction any disagreement arising out of or under the terms of this Agreement. Failing a negotiated resolution between the parties, the Organizer and the Exhibitor agree to participate in voluntary mediation (selecting a mediator by mutual agreement of the parties), but if after 60 days from the date of the first request by a party for voluntary mediation, no resolution of the dispute has occurred, then the parties agree that the dispute shall be resolved in [location], before a panel of 3 arbitrators, at least one (1) of whom shall be a lawyer with substantial commercial and art museum law experience, and in accordance with the Commercial Arbitration Rules of the American Arbitration Association in effect at the time this Agreement is signed.

B. Except to the extent that the Organizer or its representatives are negligent, the Exhibitor agrees to hold harmless, indemnify, and defend the Organizer from and against all claims, damages, losses, and expenses, including, but not limited to, reasonable attorneys' fees and disbursements, asserted against or suffered by the Organizer in connection with or arising out of this Agreement or the Exhibition or the showing of the Exhibition at the Exhibitor's location.

C. The Exhibitor agrees that in no event shall any damages payable by the Organizer as a result of a breach by it of the terms of this Agreement exceed the amount of the participation fee actually paid to the Organizer and under no circumstances shall the Exhibitor be entitled to receive, in addition to its actual damages or the refunds described above, consequential, incidental, special or punitive damages, the parties agreeing that the refund remedy set forth above, together with actual damages as limited hereby, are fair and sufficient and shall be the only remedies of the Exhibitor hereunder.

XV. Entire Agreement; Amendments

A. This Agreement and its Attachments constitute the entire understanding between the Organizer and the Exhibitor with respect to the Exhibition. This Agreement supersedes and replaces any previous documents, correspondence, conversations, and other written or oral understandings related to this Agreement.

B. This Agreement may not be amended or modified except by means of a written document, signed by both parties, and no waiver of the terms hereof shall be in effect unless in writing and signed by the party making such waiver.

XVI. Governing Law

This Agreement shall be governed by and construed, enforced, and performed in accordance with the laws of the State of [_____] without regard to conflicts of law principles.

XVII. Legal Proceedings; Seizure

If any legal actions or other legal proceedings are commenced that involve or relate to the Exhibition, and the Exhibitor or the Organizer is named as a defendant or respondent therein, the Exhibitor agrees to give prompt notice to the Organizer and to cooperate with the Organizer and with the lender, if any, of any Work that is the subject matter of such actions or proceedings in any litigation that might ensue. Should a subpoena, complaint, or other legal action or claim of ownership or right to possession be served on, asserted, or commenced against the Exhibitor or the Organizer or any of the Works, seeking to attach, obtain possession of or seize any Work in the Exhibition, the Exhibitor agrees, to the fullest extent allowed by law, to

resist such attachment or seizure and to defend itself and the Organizer and the lender, if any, of such Work, against such action or claim and, in any event, to take all steps lawfully available to the Exhibitor immediately to notify the Organizer of any attempt pursuant to such legal process to obtain possession of or seize a Work in the Exhibition before any seizure is allowed or possession of such Work is surrendered in response to such process.

XVIII. Contact Information; Notices

A. The following persons are the staff members of the Organizer and of the Exhibitor to whom inquiries and questions relating to this Agreement should be directed:

	EXHIBITOR	*ORGANIZER*
Exhibition Management/ Financial	[Name/phone/ fax/e-mail]	[Name/phone/ fax/e-mail]
Curator	[Name/phone/ fax/e-mail]	[Name/phone/ fax/e-mail]
Registrar	[Name/phone/ fax/e-mail]	[Name/phone/ fax/e-mail]
Conservator	[Name/phone/ fax/e-mail]	[Name/phone/ fax/e-mail]
Publications (Catalogs/ Brochures)	[Name/phone/ fax/e-mail]	[Name/phone/ fax/e-mail]
Publicity	[Name/phone/ fax/e-mail]	[Name/phone/ fax/e-mail]
Rights and Reproductions (including product development)	[Name/phone/ fax/e-mail]	[Name/phone/ fax/e-mail]
Sponsorship	[Name/phone/ fax/e-mail]	[Name/phone/ fax/e-mail]

B. Unless otherwise stated in this Agreement, all notices and other communications required or permitted by this Agreement shall be made

if to the Organizer, to [Name and title]

if to the Exhibitor, to [Name and title]

C. All such notices and communications shall be considered given (i) when physically delivered by hand, by courier service, by overnight delivery service, or, if by fax or email, when receipt is acknowledged; or (ii) four (4) business days after being deposited in the U.S. mail, postage paid, certified, return receipt requested.

XIX. Signatures; Binding Agreement

The Organizer and the Exhibitor each warrant to the other that the officer or officers signing this Agreement on its behalf is or are authorized to do so and that it has entered into this Agreement and caused it to be signed on its behalf, intending to be legally bound.

ORGANIZER	EXHIBITOR
By: _____	By: _____
Name: _____	Name: _____
Title: _____	Title: _____
Date: _____	Date: _____

Attachment I

Checklist of the Exhibition

Attachment II

Security

The Exhibitor will take all reasonable measures to ensure the security of the Exhibition while at its premises, including, at a minimum, the following:

1. Guard coverage and protection from the dangers of fire, smoke, water damage, loss, theft, and vandalism will be maintained 24 hours a day while the Works are on the Exhibitor's premises. All guards and security personnel shall be permanent members of the Exhibitor's staff.
2. Constant electronic security monitoring and regular patrols by security personnel will be in place; at least one guard will be deployed in each gallery at all times during public hours; guards will conduct evening/night patrols hourly if electronic coverage is inadequate in the opinion of the Organizer.
3. All entrances into the Exhibition galleries shall be secured and alarmed when the Exhibition is closed to the public.
4. All intrusion alarms shall be checked every evening to verify that they are operating properly;

nonworking alarms shall be immediately restored to service or the Exhibitor will provide alternative security, such as guards, until the alarms are restored to service.
5. Gallery alarms must report to a facility that is staffed 24 hours a day; guards who patrol the Exhibition and the Exhibitor's premises at night must be in radio or telephone contact with this facility at all times.
6. Alarms for individual Works will be used if used elsewhere at the Exhibitor's facility.
7. All alarms and monitoring devices shall have a backup power supply that will maintain the operation of these units for a minimum of 4 hours.
8. Security screws must be used for hanging all Works.
9. No visiting copyists or students are permitted to work in the Exhibition galleries with wet media.
10. No eating, drinking, or smoking will be allowed in any Exhibition galleries.

Attachment III

Photographs and Publicity

1. The Organizer will provide a selection of 8 × 10-inch black-and-white photographs, color slides, and 4 × 5-inch color transparencies to the Exhibitor for use in promotional and educational materials for the Exhibition, but the costs for any new photography requested by the Exhibitor will be borne by the Exhibitor.
2. Photographs provided by the Organizer and approved for promotional and educational reproduction must be accompanied by full documentation including ownership credit. The copyright designation (where relevant) must be printed immediately under or beside the reproduction. Documentation should include artist's name, title of Work, date, medium, size, and lender credit. The Exhibitor will provide this information to news media.
3. Images reproduced from black-and-white photographs or negatives, color transparencies, or slides, whether for promoting the Exhibition or any other purpose, may not be cropped or bled off the page, printed in any single color other than black, nor may anything be superimposed on the image without submitting a design to the Organizer for approval. Images used on the Exhibitor's website, however, must be watermarked by the Exhibitor before being posted. For review purposes, the Exhibitor must

notify the Organizer when such images are posted on the Exhibitor's website.

4. At the close of the Exhibition, the Exhibitor will send the following materials and information (the Publicity Report) to the attention of the Organizer's Exhibitions Manager (the costs of supplying the report will be borne by the Exhibitor) no later than [_] days after the Exhibition closes at the Exhibitor's location:

a. attendance figures for the Exhibition;

b. two (2) sets of color slides of the installation (minimum: five views); one set taken during public hours and one set while the galleries are empty;

c. two (2) sets of black-and-white photographs of the Exhibition opening or other special events (minimum: five views);

d. two (2) copies of each piece of printed matter produced by the Exhibitor in connection with the Exhibition, such as publicity posters, brochures, checklists, press releases, invitations, and any other material relating to the Exhibition;

e. two (2) copies of press clippings of reviews and articles about the Exhibition from newspapers and magazines;

f. two (2) copies of each print ad;

g. one (1) copy of each videotape or cassette tape produced by the Exhibitor for use by local media in publicizing the Exhibition;

h. one (1) copy of each television or radio program in which the Exhibition received coverage, if the Exhibitor has obtained copies of such for its own use;

i. addresses of any websites where information and/or images relating to the Exhibition has been posted;

j. an outline or checklist of the publicity sought or obtained for the Exhibition; and

k. any other similar relevant material relating to the Exhibition and the publicity for the Exhibition.

Prepared for "Exhibition Contracts: A Roadmap for Collaboration and Cooperation," AAM Annual Meeting, Baltimore, May 16, 2000. Panelists Katherine Solender, Exhibitions Manager, The Cleveland Museum of Art; Ann B. Robertson, Exhibition Officer, National Gallery of Art; Patricia Loiko, Registrar, Museum of Fine Arts, Boston; and Stephen J. Knerly, Esq., Hahn Loeser & Parks LLP, Cleveland.

Sample Incoming Loan Agreement

THE SAMPLER MUSEUM
123 Any Street, Any Town, Any State

Telephone: 000-000-0001

INCOMING LOAN AGREEMENT

AGREEMENT	The undersigned ("Lender") hereby lends to The Sampler Museum the object(s) described herein for the purposes, and subject to the terms and conditions set forth.
EXHIBITION	Exhibition: Dates: Venues: Sampler Museum Registrar:
LENDER	Lender: Address: Contact Person: Telephone: (business) (home) Mobile: Credit: Lent by_____ —— (Indicate exact wording of Lender's name for catalog, labels, and publicity)
OBJECT	Artist/Maker: Object/Title: Medium: Date of Work:

DIMENSIONS

Painting/Print	height in.	width	in. (unframed)			
	height in.	width	in.		depth	in. (framed)
Object	height in.	width	in.		depth	in.
	approximate weight		lbs.			

May we reframe, remat, or remount if necessary for the safety of the work? _____ Yes _____No

May we substitute Plexiglas for glass? _____Yes _____No

May we affix secure hanging devices onto frame? _____Yes _____No

INSURANCE Please see reverse for conditions	Total value (estimated Current Market Value in US $): _____ The Sampler Museum will insure unless otherwise advised. Do you prefer to maintain your own insurance? ____Yes ____No If yes, estimated cost of premium: US$_____ Do you require a certificate of insurance? ____Yes ____No
PHOTOGRAPHY Please see reverse for conditions	If black-and-white photographs and/or color transparencies suitable for reproduction are available, please state type and where they may obtained.
SHIPPING/ HANDLING	Date required for receipt of loan at The Sampler Museum: _____ Pick-up and/or return address, if different from address above. ____Pick-up ____ Return Address: Name of contact if other than Lender: Telephone: (business) (home) (mobile) Please list any special instructions for handling, packing, shipping, or installation:
SIGNATURE	The Lender acknowledges that he/she has full authority and power to make this loan, that he/she has read the conditions above and on the reverse of this form, and that he/she agrees to be bound by them.

Signature: _____   Date: _____
        Lender or authorized agent

Signature: _____   Date: _____
        For The Sampler Museum

Please complete, sign and return both copies to The Sampler Museum Registrar. A countersigned copy will be sent to you.

CONDITIONS GOVERNING INCOMING LOANS

CARE AND HANDLING

1. The Sampler Museum (the "Museum") will exercise the same care with respect to the work of art on loan (the "work") as it does with comparable property of its own.

2. The Museum will not alter, clean, or repair the work without prior express written permission of the Lender or except when the safety of the work makes such action imperative.

PACKING AND TRANSPORTATION

1. The Lender certifies that the work is in good condition and will withstand ordinary strains of packing and transportation. Evidence of damage to the work at the time of receipt or while in the Museum's custody will be reported immediately to the Lender. The work will be returned packed in the same or similar materials unless otherwise authorized by the Lender. Costs of transportation and packing will be borne by the Museum unless the loan is at the Lender's request. Customs regulations will be adhered to in international shipments.

INSURANCE

1. Unless the Lender expressly elects to maintain his/her own insurance coverage, the Museum will insure the work wall-to-wall under its fine arts policy against risks of physical loss or damage from external cause while in transit and on location during the period of the loan. The insurance coverage contains the usual exclusions of loss or damage due to such causes as wear and tear, gradual deterioration, moths, vermin, inherent vice, war, invasion, hostilities, insurrections, nuclear reaction or radiation, confiscation by order of any government or public authority, risk of contraband or illegal transportation and/or trade, and any repairing, restoration or retouching authorized by the Lender.

2. Insurance will be placed in the amount specified by the Lender, which must reflect fair market value. In case of damage or loss, the insurance company may ask the Lender to substantiate the insurance value. If the Lender fails to indicate an amount, the Museum will set a value for purposes of insurance only for the period of the loan. The United States Government Arts and Artifacts Indemnity Act may be applicable to this loan. If so, the Lender agrees to said coverage at US dollar valuation as specified in this loan agree-

ment. If a work that has been industrially fabricated is damaged or lost and can be repaired or replaced to the artist's specifications, the Museum's liability shall be limited to the cost of such replacement. The Lender agrees that in the event of loss or damage, recovery shall be limited to such amount, if any, as may be paid by the insurer, hereby releasing the Museum and the Trustees, officers, agents, and employees of the Museum from liability for any and all claims arising out of such loss or damage.

3. If the Lender chooses to maintain his or her own insurance, the Museum must be supplied with a certificate of insurance naming the Museum as an additional insured or waiving subrogation against the Museum. If the Lender fails to supply the Museum with such a certificate, this loan agreement shall constitute a release of the Museum from any liability in connection with the work. The Museum cannot accept responsibility for any error in the information furnished to the Lender's insurer or for any lapses in coverage.

REPRODUCTION AND CREDIT

1. The Museum assumes the right, unless specifically denied by the Lender, to photograph, videotape, and reproduce the work for documentation, publicity, publication, and educational purposes connected with this exhibition and to produce slides of the work to be distributed for educational use.

2. The general public will not be allowed to photograph works on loan to The Sampler Museum.

3. Unless otherwise instructed in writing, the Museum will give credit to the Lender in any labels and publications as specified on the face of the agreement.

OWNERSHIP AND CHANGE IN OWNERSHIP

1. The Lender hereby warrants that he/she has full legal title to the work or that he/she is the duly authorized agent of the owner or owners of the work. The Lender will indemnify, defend, and hold the Museum harmless from any losses, damages, and expenses, including attorney's fees, arising out of claims by individuals, institutions or other persons claiming full or partial title to the work.

2. The Lender will notify the Museum promptly in writing of any change of ownership of the work whether by reason of death, sale, insolvency, gift, or otherwise. If ownership shall change during the period of this loan, the Museum reserves the right to require the new owner, prior to the return of the

work, to establish his or her right to possession by proof satisfactory to the Museum. The new owner shall succeed to Lender's rights and obligations under this agreement, including, but not limited to, the loan period and any insurance obligations.

LOAN PERIOD, EXTENSION, RETURN

1. The work shall remain in the possession of the Museum for the time specified on the reverse, but may be withdrawn from exhibition at any time by the Museum. The Lender agrees that he/she cannot withdraw the work during the period of this agreement without prior written consent of the Museum Director.

2. The terms of this agreement shall apply to any extension of the loan period.

3. Unless the Lender requests otherwise in writing, the Museum will return the work only to the Lender and only at the address specified in this agreement. The Lender shall promptly notify the Museum in writing of any change of address. The Museum assumes no responsibility to search for a Lender who cannot be reached at the address specified in this agreement. The Lender will pay additional costs, if any, if the Lender requests the return of the work to another address.

4. The Museum's right to return the loan shall accrue absolutely at the termination of the loan. If, after pursuing all possible means of contact, and in accordance with any legal requirements, the Lender cannot be found or the Lender refuses to accept the return of the work, it shall be deemed abandoned and become the property of the Museum. [This clause must comply with state law.]

INTERPRETATION

1. This agreement constitutes the entire agreement between the Lender and the Museum and may be amended or modified only in writing signed by both parties. Any changes herein of printed text or written additions must bear the initial of both parties. This agreement shall be governed and interpreted according to the laws of the State of Any State.

2. If the terms of this agreement conflict with the forms, agreements, or correspondence of the Lender, the terms of this agreement will be controlling.

Sample Incoming Receipt

THE SAMPLER MUSEUM
123 Any Street, Any Town, Any State

Telephone: 000-000-0001

INCOMING RECEIPT

The objects described below, or on attached pages, have been received by The Sampler Museum and are subject to the terms and conditions set forth below and on the reverse.

Received from:

Name (Depositor)	Owner's name (if different)
Street address	Street address
City, state, zip code	City, state, zip code
Business telephone	Business telephone
Home telephone	Home telephone
Mobile telephone	Mobile telephone

Purpose of
Deposit: _____

Date received: _____

Museum Reference Number	Description

The conditions and terms of this incoming receipt, as stated above and on the reverse side hereof, are accepted in full by the depositor.

Received by: _____
Signature for The Sampler Museum   Date

_____
Name and title

Depositor: _____
Signature of depositor or authorized agent Date

_____
Name and title

CONDITIONS UNDER WHICH OBJECTS ARE RECEIVED

CARE AND HANDLING

1. The Sampler Museum (the "Museum") will give objects left in its custody the same care as it does to comparable property of its own, but will assume no additional responsibilities in regard to such objects. It is understood by the Depositor that all tangible objects are subject to gradual inherent deterioration for which the Museum is not responsible.

2. The absence of condition notes on this receipt does not imply that the objects were received in good condition.

3. The Museum will not clean, restore, reframe, or otherwise alter the objects without the written consent of the Depositor. If such work has been authorized, the cost will be subject to special written agreement between the Depositor and the Museum.

4. Attributions, dates, and other information shown overleaf are as given by the Depositor. Any valuations or prices shown are those stated by the Depositor and are not to be construed as appraisals by the Museum. The fact that the objects have been in the Museum's custody shall not be misused to indicate the Museum's endorsement.

5. The Museum will not provide transportation for objects deposited with it unless special arrangements are agreed to in writing by the Museum. When objects are returned to the Depositor pursuant to such arrangements, failure to sign and return the official Museum outgoing receipt within 30 days of shipment of said objects shall release the Museum from any liability for the said objects.

INSURANCE

1. The Depositor hereby releases the Museum, its agents, and employees, from liability for any and all claims arising out of loss or damage to such objects. Unless a signed loan agreement stating terms of the loan and insurance exists, the Museum is not responsible for insurance coverage of the deposited objects

PHOTOGRAPHY

1. Unless the Museum is notified in writing to the contrary, the Depositor agrees that the objects covered by this receipt may be photographed for record, publicity or educational purposes. Such photographs will not be published or sold to the public without written consent of the Depositor.

RETURNS

1. The Museum will give reasonable notice in writing if it desires to return any object to the Depositor; and the Museum will make reasonable efforts to return the object to the Depositor.

If such efforts are unavailing for any reason, the right of the Museum to require the Depositor to withdraw the said object shall accrue absolutely on the date of and by mailing a notice to the address listed overleaf via certified mail. If the Depositor does not withdraw the loan within sixty days from the date of such notice, then the Museum may charge regular storage fees and enforce a lien for the fees. If after five years the loan is not withdrawn, and in consideration for its storage and safeguarding during this period, it shall be deemed an unrestricted gift to the Museum. [This clause must be written according to state law.]

2. Objects covered by this receipt that are not included as loan items in an exhibition then on exhibit may be removed from the Museum by the Depositor or his or her duly authorized agent or successor in interest after reasonable notice upon surrender of this receipt or the delivery of the Depositor's written order. Unless other arrangements have been approved in writing by the Museum, objects will be returned only to the Depositor at the address stated overleaf.

3. In the event that an object, the ownership having meanwhile passed by sale, bequest, or gift, is not to be returned to the original Depositor, the new owner or recipient must establish, in advance of such return, his or her authority to receive it to the satisfaction of the Museum's counsel.

WARRANTY OF TITLE

1. The Depositor warrants that he or she is the owner of the object, that the object is not subject to ownership claims of any other person, institution, or domestic or foreign governments, and that all applicable domestic and foreign customs and export/import regulations have been complied with.

If the Depositor is not the owner of the objects, the Depositor warrants that he or she has full authority to enter into this deposit transaction on behalf of the owner, and the owner is fully bound hereby as the Depositor's principal. The Museum may require written evidence of the Depositor's agency satisfactory in form to its counsel.

Selected Bibliography

PUBLICATIONS

Bentley, Andres. "New special provision for international shipping of natural history specimens." *SPNHC Newsletter* 25(1):1–9, 2011.

Bogle, Elizabeth. *Museum Exhibition. Planning and Design.* Lanham, MD: Altamira Press, 2013.

Bray, Alida J. "Guidelines for Resource Management of Traveling Exhibitions." Unpublished thesis, John F. Kennedy University, September 1995.

Buck, Rebecca A., and Jean Allman Gilmore, eds. *MRM5: Museum Registration Methods*, 5th ed. Washington, DC: American Association of Museums Press, 2010.

Case, Mary. *Registrars on Record: Essays on Museums Collections Management.* Washington, DC: American Association of Museums Press, 1988.

Cincinnati Museum of Natural History. *Exhibit Topic Survey for Museum Colleagues*, 1993.

Danziger and Danziger. *Art Newspaper March 2002.* New York.

Dawson, Vicky, and Allison Hecker. "Hidden legacies in traveling exhibitions." *Exhibition. A Journal of Exhibition Theory & Practice for Museum Professionals*, Spring 2012:24–29.

Fell, Rebecca J. "Designing traveling exhibitions for the small community." *Exhibition. A Journal of Exhibition Theory & Practice for Museum Professionals*, Spring 2012:74–77.

Gilbert, Courtney, and Norma Henry. "Traveling exhibition at the end of it run? Now what?" *Exhibition. A Journal of Exhibition Theory & Practice for Museum Professionals*, Spring 2012:70–73.

Goldowsky, Alexander, and Betsy Loring. "Collaborative structures: many ways, common paths." *Exhibition. A Journal of Exhibition Theory & Practice for Museum Professionals*, Spring 2012:14–15.

Imholte, Joe, Heather Farnworth, Charity Counts, and Whitney Owens. "From hall to hallway: taking a permanent exhibition on the road." *Exhibition. A Journal of Exhibition Theory & Practice for Museum Professionals*, Spring 2012:56–60.

Johnson, Arne P., W. Robert Hannen, and Frank Zuccari. "Vibration control during museum construction projects." *Journal of the American Institute for Conservation* 52(1) 2013:30–47.

Jones, Michael E. *Art Law. A Concise Guide for Artists, Curators, and Art Educators.* Lanham, MD: Rowman & Littlefield, 2016.

Malaro, Marie C., and Ildiko P. DeAngelis. *A Legal Primer on Managing Museum Collections*, 3rd ed. Washington, DC: Smithsonian Books, 2012.

Michalski, Stefan. "Stuffing everything we know about mechanical properties into one collection simulation." *Climate for Collections: Standards and Uncertainties.* Munich: Doerner Institute/Archetype Publications Ltd., 2013.

PACIN. *Packing and Crating Information Network Notebook* (Conference Notebook, April 25, 1992. Baltimore, MD). Compiled and edited by Scott Atthowe and Michael Smallwood, 1992.

PACIN. *Technical Drawing Handbook of Packing and Crating Methods.* Compiled by Packing and Crating Information Network, American Association of Museums, Registrars Committee Task Force, 1993.

Pearson, Paul. "Greater than its parts: exhibition collaborations for small museums." *Exhibition. A Journal of Exhibition Theory & Practice for Museum Professionals*, Spring 2012:8–13.

Phelan, Marilyn E. *Museum Law. A Guide for Officers, Directors, and Counsel*, 4th ed. Lanham, MD: Rowman & Littlefield, 2014.

Pollock, Wendy. "The shadow side of traveling exhibitions." *Exhibition. A Journal of Exhibition Theory & Practice for Museum Professionals*, Spring 2012:62–67.

Powell, Brent. *Collection Care, An Illustrated Handbook for the Care and Handling of Cultural Objects.* Lanham, MD: Rowman & Littlefield, 2015.

Rose, Cordelia. *Courierspeak.* Washington, DC: Smithsonian Institution Press, 1993.

Ruiz, Agnés. "Five challenges for marketing traveling exhibitions to professionals." *Exhibition. A Journal of Exhibition Theory & Practice for Museum Professionals*, Spring 2012:46–49.

Ryan, Kathleen, Kathy Dawes, and Dana Dawes. "Boxed and ready to travel: taking learning on the road." *Exhibition. A Journal of Exhibition Theory & Practice for Museum Professionals*, Spring 2012:40–45.

Schillace-Nelson, Mia. "Traveling exhibitions feature live animals: Are they for you?" *Exhibition. A Journal of Exhibition Theory & Practice for Museum Professionals*, Spring 2012:52–55.

Serrell, Beverly. *Exhibit Labels. An Interpretive Approach*, 2nd ed. Lanham, MD: Rowman & Littlefield, 2015.

Sixsmith, Mike, ed. *Touring Exhibitions: The Touring Exhibition Group's Manual of Good Practice*. Oxford, UK: Butterworth-Heineman Ltd., 1995.

Stryker, Tams, and Dill. *Legal Issues for Museum Administrators,* workshop, The Newark Museum, September 13, 1995. Mid-Atlantic Association of Museums and New Jersey Association of Museums.

Stuart, R. Wallace. "Immunity from Judicial Seizure of Cultural Objects Imported for Temporary Exhibition," study materials for ALI-ABA's *Legal Problems of Museum Administration*, 1997.

Thickett, David. "Vibration damage levels for museum objects." *13th Triennial Meeting, Rio de Janeiro Preprints*, 2002. Vol. 1, 90–95.

Thomas, Geri. *Traveling Exhibitions from A to Z: Coming to a Community Near You.* Unpublished material for Traveling Exhibitions PIC workshop, Dallas, Texas, May 2002.

Tirrell, Peter. *Strategic Planning for Traveling Exhibitions.* Unpublished material for Traveling Exhibitions PIC workshop, Dallas, Texas, May 2002.

Witteborg, Lothar P. *Good Show! A Practical Guide for Temporary Exhibitions*, 2nd ed. Washington, DC; Smithsonian Institution Traveling Exhibition Service, 1991.

WEBSITES OF INTEREST

[Accessed and updated, October 2019]

Arts and Artifacts Indemnity Program. Available at: https://www.arts.gov/artistic-fields/museums/arts-and-artifacts-indemnity-program-international-indemnity

Association of Registrars and Collection Specialists (ARCS). Available at: https://www.arcsinfo.org/

Convention on the Means of Prohibiting and Preventing the Illicit Import, Export and Transfer of Ownership of Cultural Property (UNESCO Convention), 1970. Available at: http://portal.unesco.org/en/ev.php-URL_ID=13039&URL_DO=DO_TOPIC&URL_SECTION=201.html

Convention on Cultural Property Implementation Act (CCPIA), 1983. Available at: https://eca.state.gov/files/bureau/97-446.pdf

Convention on International Trade in Endangered Species of Wild Fauna and Flora (CITES). Available at: http://www.cites.org/

General Facility Report (formerly Standard Facility Report). American Alliance of Museums, 2011, rev. Available at: https://ww2.aam-us.org/ProductCatalog/Product?ID=891

Immunity from Seizure under Judicial Process of Cultural Objects Imported for Temporary Exhibition or Display. Available at: https://www.state.gov/immunity-from-judicial-seizure-statute-22-u-s-c-2459/

Importation of Pre-Columbian Monumental or Architectural Sculpture or Murals Act (Pre-Columbian Art Act), 1972. Available at: https://www.law.cornell.edu/uscode/text/19/chapter-11

Lacey Act, 1900. Available at: http://www.fws.gov/le/pdf files/Lacey.pdf

Preparation Art Handling, Collections Care Information Network (PACCIN). Available at: http://www.paccin.org

Standards for Museum Exhibitions and Indicators of Excellence, 2012. Professional Networks Council, American Alliance of Museums. Available at: https://static1.squarespace.com/static/58fa260a725e25c4f30020f3/t/58ff73ed3e00bea8e746d4ce/1493136367751/2012+Standards+for+Museum++Exhibitions+and+Indicators+of+Excellence.pdf

UNIDROIT Convention on Stolen or Illegally Exported Cultural Objects, 1995. Available at: https://www.unidroit.org/102-instruments/cultural-property/cultural-property-convention-1995/173-unidroit-convention-on-stolen-or-illegally-exported-cultural-objects-1995-rome

Visual Artists Rights Act (VARA) 1990. Available at: http://www.law.harvard.edu/faculty/martin/art_law/esworthy.htm

Index

About the Authors

Jean Allman Gilmore and **Rebecca A. Buck** served as coeditors of the AAM Registrars Committee (RC-AAM) journal *REGISTRAR* from 1987 to 1993. They both served, at different times, as vice chair, then chair, of the Mid-Atlantic Association of Museums Registrars Committee (MAAM-RC). They are co-editors of *The New Museum Registration Methods*, published by AAM in 1998, and were named co-recipients of the Dudley-Wilkinson Award of Distinction in 2001. In 2010, they coedited *MRM5*, the fifth edition of *Museum Registration Methods*. They both became founding directors of the Association of Registrars and Collections Specialists (ARCS) in 2011. Following their retirements in 2013, they formed Buck & Gilmore, LLC, offering art and artifact management solutions to museums and collectors.

Rebecca A. Buck retired as deputy director for Collection Services and chief registrar at the Newark Museum, Newark, New Jersey. She was formerly registrar at the Hood Museum of Art, Dartmouth College (1982–1990) and at the University of Pennsylvania Museum of Archaeology and Anthropology, Philadelphia (1990–1995). She was curator of collections at the Cheney Cowles Memorial Museum (now Northwest Museum of Arts & Culture) in Spokane, Washington, from 1975 to 1982. She holds degrees from Oberlin College and Boston University and taught in the museum professions program at Seton Hall University. Rebecca has been a MAP II surveyor and chaired RC-AAM (2000–2002) and the Standing Professional Committee Council (2001–2001). Rebecca is an avid birder and a lover of cacophonous music.

Jean Allman Gilmore retired after thirty-one years as registrar of the Brandywine River Museum, Chadds Ford, Pennsylvania. She earned a BA from Wittenberg University and an MA from the University of Wyoming and completed the museum studies program at the University of Delaware. In addition to serving as chair of MAAM-RC, she was secretary of the MAAM Board of Governors. Jean served two terms as vice president of ARCS. She spends her free time knitting, studying Italian, and playing with her dogs and cat.

Irene Taurins is Director of Registration at the Philadelphia Museum of Art where she has worked since 1978. She oversees the documentation and movement of works of art into, out of, and within the museum, physically and legally. She has organized and circulated many special exhibitions. Irene was a founding director of the ARCS and served as corresponding secretary for three years. She wrote the chapter on "Shipping" for *The New Museum Registration Methods* in 1998 and for *Museum Registration Methods*, 5th edition in 2010 and 6th edition in 2020. She has been a courier on many occasions, including an "around-the-world" courier trip from Philadelphia to Toronto to Taipei to Paris and back to Philadelphia in one week. Prior to joining the Philadelphia Museum of Art, Irene was the registrar/administrator at Sotheby's, New York, where she was instrumental in introducing and implementing new forms and procedures for inventory control of works of art. When she is not registering, she enjoys travel and warm water snorkeling.

CPSIA information can be obtained
at www.ICGtesting.com
Printed in the USA
BVHW010012050620
580710BV00016B/520